Population Theory
in China

Population
Theory
in
China

Edited with an introduction
by H. Yuan Tien

M. E. Sharpe, Inc. *White Plains, New York*
Croom Helm *London*

#9646015957
#76391315

First published in Great Britain 1980
by Croom Helm Ltd
2-10 St John's Road, London SW11

Published simultaneously as Vol. X, No. 1, of *International Journal of
Politics*. Selections from *Renkou lilun* were translated by H. Yuan Tien.

Library of Congress Catalog Card Number: 79-57159
M. E. Sharpe, Inc. ISBN: 0-87332-174-X
Croom Helm ISBN: 0-7099-0444-4

Printed in the United States of America

Contents

Continued

Preface

The People's Republic of China is thirty years young, but her people have an experience extending more than 2,000 years into the past. From both a personal and professional point of view, however, 1979 alone has brought enough major events to easily fill pages and pages. The once seemingly unbridgeable gap between China and the U.S. was formally bridged early in this Year of Normalization. Deng Xiaoping, the Senior Deputy Premier, visited Washington, D.C., in January, and Walter Mondale, the Vice-President, paid a return visit to Beijing in September. I was able to be on hand and partake in formal events in honor of these official visitors in both cities.

I mention these two happy and significant occasions because they are part of the rapidly unfolding circumstances that made the birth of this translated work possible and pleasurable. These developing events include a short trip to China that I along with several other members of the Population Association of America made in April 1978. In twelve days we traversed China's vast space. One of the brief stops was Shanghai, where three other members of the group and I walked the streets in preference to a one-day excursion to the nearby city of Suzhou. In the Xinhua Bookstore on Nanjing Road, I spotted and immediately bought a copy of *Renkou lilun*. Although the book has a December 1977 publication date, that was the first time I had ever known of its existence. A couple of days later in Beijing, we tried to get in touch with the authors of the book, who were then on the staff of the Office of Population Research, Beijing College of Economics. However, contact was limited to the indirect presentation, via the Beijing Office of China's International Travel Service, of 46 volumes of *Demography* that we had collectively lugged across the Pacific on behalf of the Population Association of America.

But, in the few months interval after that, there had occurred in rapid succession additional far-reaching changes that have since generated a great many opportunities for direct contacts at all levels. An agreement was signed in October 1978 between China's Scientific and Technical Association and the U.S. Committee on Scholarly Communication with the People's Republic of China. This agreement sets forth, among other things, the terms of the Senior Scholar Program in 1979-1980, under which I was able to return to China for research in the summer of 1979.

Over the years since the late 1940s, numerous Chinese books, documents, articles, etc. have been translated into English by scholars in the U.S. Insofar as I know, few of the translators have ever had the opportunity to meet the original writers of the translated items. In April 1979 I was notified by the U.S. Committee of my selection as one of the fifteen Senior Scholars to undertake research in China for the first time in thirty years. Not only has this action paved the way for my present research sojourn in China, but it has also made it possible for me to become personally acquainted with the authors of *Renkou lilun*. I very much appreciate the Committee's support. I want to thank the authors, Liu Zheng, Wu Cangping, Feng Litian, Zhai Shiguang, Hou Wenro, Yu Tiao, Zhou Qing, Wang Nairong, Cha Ruichuan, Lin Fude and Li Gen, for their acquiescent blessing of this English version of their joint product.

In China, the summer months of 1979 turned out to be a uniquely exciting time in many other ways as well. For the first time since the late 1950s, the National Planning Bureau gave out a specific population figure for the country as a whole: as of the end of 1978, there were 975,230,000 people in the whole nation (Taiwan included). In Beijing, Shanghai, and Tianjin, scholars in various universities and others in the social sciences and in family planning formed population institutes in their respective municipalities in preparation for the more orderly exchange of views and for more systematic research.

The deposal of the "gang of four" has indeed meant a renaissance in demographic studies in China. The foremost symbol of this reemergence and expansion of population research has been the reversal of the verdict in the case of Professor Ma Yinchu. All through the summer months since early July, newspapers have given extensive coverage of the injustice and mistreatment that this distinguished scholar received during the preceding twenty years, and of his renowned "New Population Theory." In this treatise, once condemned as bourgeois and Malthusian, Professor Ma had argued that on the basis of China's population size and trends of the early 1950s, the country could ill afford an uncontrolled growth of more than 2 percent per annum, and that in order to accelerate industrialization, population increase must be controlled to raise the rate of capital accumulation and to lower consumption. Specifically, he recommended that contraception and late marriage be promoted and that, if these were insufficient, they be supplemented by "more stern and more effective administrative measures" (*Guangming ribao*, July 26, 1979). In September, Professor Ma was made an honorary President of Beijing University, a post from which he had been ousted in 1960.

In August, Chen Muhua, Deputy Premier and head of the State Council's Planned Reproduction Leading Group, formally announced the institution of various measures designed to curb fertility and the possibility of peanalizing couples in case of fertility excesses. A campaign to promote single-birth families is also being widely pushed. The announced aim is to reduce the rate of natural increase to 5 per 1000 by 1985, when, it is expected, all births will be of either first or second parity throughout the nation. I have, therefore, been a witness to not only the symbolic restoration of Professor Ma's reputation and standing, but also the acceptance of the substantive points of his "New Population Theory." To be able to be on the spot to see these monumental and momentous changes is one of the most gratifying things I have ever experienced. It has made the proofreading of the galleys a joy.

All this has been facilitated by a grant from the Ford and Rockefeller Foundations under their Population and Development Policy Research Program for 1979-1980. This, coupled with a research leave from the Department of Sociology, The Ohio State University, has made it financially possible for me to spend an extended period of time at the most opportune moment in China. I would like to mention specifically Dr. Mary Kritz of the Rockefeller Foundation for her interest in and encouragement of population studies relating to China. My deepest gratitude goes to her.

Josephine A. Matthews patiently read the rough draft and made numerous improvements. I want to thank her for this invaluable help and for other spousal aid and comfort in the course of this translation.

Cindy Brown cheerfully typed the manuscript, and Laurie Taress conscientiously prepared the appendices. To them I wish to express deep appreciation. Yu Shen of Beijing Friendship Hotel did the calligraphy on the cover.

Lastly, I want to thank Douglas Merwin of M. E. Sharpe, Inc. for his prompt attention and assistance in getting this book published within a very short period of time.

H.Y.T.
Beijing, October 1, 1979
The Thirtieth Anniversary of
the People's Republic of China

Population Theory in China

Introduction

H. Yuan Tien

During the thirty years since its proclamation in 1949, the People's Republic of China has more or less successfully managed the country's demographic affairs under the most adverse circumstances. Also, the years 1949 to 1979 stand out, demographically, as the most momentous period in China's history: reportedly some 300 million people (that is, almost one and one-half times the total population of the United States) have been added to the population since the 1953 Census of China, which showed a total population of 588 million. The salience and implications of China's ability to manage its demographic affairs thus are rendered more profound by this unprecedented population growth.

Of course, all this is not to suggest that the last thirty years have been free of controversies. In fact, precise information on population patterns and trends in the People's Republic of China is in short supply. The shortage is such that high officials in China have given varied versions of population increases in recent years. At the ECAFE meeting that was held in April 1973, Chi Lung, deputy representative of the Chinese Delegation, stated that "over the past twenty-four years, China's population grew from more than 500 million to over 700 million, an increase of more than 50 percent" (see Appendix D). A little more than a year later, on August 21, 1974, Huang Shu-tse, head of the Chinese Delegation to the United Nations World Population Conference, reported that "in the twenty odd years since the founding of the People's Republic, China's population has increased nearly 60 percent, from about 500 million to nearly 800 million" (Appendix F). The size of the Chinese population thus has been and remains only very imprecisely established. This imprecision, coupled with the absence of birth and death data of nationwide coverage, has inevitably provided ample room for disagreements among foreign observers of China's population developments.

Notwithstanding, or in spite of, significant uncertainties with regard to demographic events in China, the Chinese struggle over their population problem is an irresistible issue in the contemporary world because of the simple fact that it involves one-fifth of the human race. Unfortunately, owing to a paucity of data and in response to demands for current demographic information, almost invariably speculation and conjecture on China's population patterns and trends have been resorted to in estimating or projecting the size and growth of the Chinese population. The estimates and projections thus fabricated have, for this very reason, been variously colored by the personal and political biases of their makers. As a result, data derived from efforts of this kind have stagflated: the output of numbers printed and circulated has undergone a manyfold increase, but their power to purchase understanding has, if anything, diminished.

For example, the size of the Chinese population in 1975 has been estimated to be from 825 to 930 million by different estimators, China's crude birthrate from 14 to 37 per 1000 inhabitants, the crude death rate from 6 to 13 per 1000, and the rate of natural increase from .8 percent to 2.4 percent per year. The wide range of these estimates serves only to confuse the Chinese demographic picture. Apart from this, one population expert also wonders whether any further insights can really be gained by figuring out, in the absence of hard data, if the size of the Chinese population and the various vital rates are within the estimated ranges (Frejka, 1976).

The many controversies surrounding China's demographic course and circumstances probably cannot be settled for a long time to come. China has yet to collect and publish population data needed for settling the issues.

Notwithstanding this relative inaction in the area of population statistics, there can be no doubt that China has done much to influence the course of the country's population trends. Since 1949, more explicit population measures have been adopted and implemented than in any other similar time interval in China's history. Taken as a whole, the last thirty years should go down in history as the watershed in the management of China's demographic affairs. This is particularly true in the area of controlling population growth. Here, the government and the Communist Party have devised and put into effect measures that had been neither known nor tried in pre-1949 China.

As a matter of fact, few countries in the modern world have done as much as the People's Republic of China has done in this regard. On March 5, 1978, for instance, the Fifth National People's Congress adopted a new Constitution of the People's Republic of China. The third and last paragraph of Article 53 of the Constitution reads, "The State advocates and encourages family planning."

The inclusion of family planning in a national constitution is a rare practice among modern nations. In this particular case, it followed the remarks of Chairman Hua Guofeng before the People's Congress on February 26 that

> family planning is a very significant matter. Planned control of population growth is conducive to the planned development of the national economy and to the health of mother and child. It also benefits the people where production, work and study are concerned. We must continue to give it serious attention and strive to lower the annual rate of growth of China's population to less than 1 percent within three years. (Hua, 1978)

The highest governmental unit for family planning work in China is the State Council's Planned Birth Staff Office (also known as the Planned Birth Leading Group), which came into existence in the mid-1960s. Shortly after the constitutional endorsement of family planning, the Planned Birth Staff Office convened a conference, the first on family planning work in China, to study ways of reducing fertility to the level specified in Hua's remarks. The conference lasted from June 26 to 28 and was followed by the reconstitution and expansion of the Office. Headed by Chen Muhua since July 7, 1978, the new Planned Birth Staff Office has thirty-three members (*People's Daily*, July 9, 1978). A national conference on family planning is being organized by the State Council to take place some time in 1979.

The purpose of the forthcoming national conference on family planning is to enable family planning units and personnel at different levels to exchange experiences and to advance education, research, and policy implementation in the area of planned birth.

Family planning thus is being publicly, positively, and strongly pursued in China. It has been reported that the rate of natural increase has steadily declined in recent years and dropped to below 1 percent per year in such cities and provinces as Beijing, Shanghai, Tianjin, Sichuan, Hebei, Liaoning, Shandong, Jiangsu, and Hubei (*Ibid.*). In other words, and as numerous visitors to the People's Republic of China have also reported, China has achieved a measure of success in fertility reduction and is seeking to achieve further decreases throughout the country, particularly in the villages. (Tien, 1975)

But there is much more to the inception and intensification of family planning activities in China than the above-mentioned endorsements and reported achievements make evident. Family planning activities started sometime in the mid-1950s, and have ebbed and flowed over the years (Tien, 1973, for discussion of earlier developments). Controversies consequently have arisen among observers over the course of, and the circumstances surrounding, the activities in this area. As in the case of China's population size and growth, discussions and analyses of China's actions in the area of family planning have had to be based on intermittent and incomplete disclosures of their details. Although a good deal of information was available in 1956-57 which permitted a relatively clear appreciation of the rationale and scope of China's family planning activities at the time, the many controversies over the Chinese effort to reduce fertility have their roots in the much diminished flow of relevant data in the 1960s and the early 1970s.

During those years reports of family planning activities in China were often indirect and unobtrusive. The most notable exception was a remark by the late Premier Zhou Enlai to Edgar Snow in January 1964 that

> we do believe in planned parenthood, but it is not easy to introduce it all at once in China, and it is more difficult to achieve in rural areas, where most of our people live, than in the cities. . . . (*The New York Times*, February 3, 1964)

Since then, various pronouncements have been made by Chinese officials attending international conferences on population and related matters. These have shed some light on China's efforts to reduce population growth. Overall, however, recent pronouncements amount to no more than a few bits of critical information. Much more is required to make it possible to account for China's recent successes in fertility reduction and to answer questions concerning the past and future course of family planning activities in China.

Renkou lilun

Thus, it is especially welcome and exciting that the Office of Population Research of the Peking College of Economics* published, in December 1977, a jointly authored volume entitled *Renkou lilun* (Population Theory), three chapters of which I have translated in the present book. In this 211-page work is the first systematic and fairly comprehensive disclosure since the 1950s of how China has viewed the need for, and gone about implementing, the control of rapid population growth in recent years. On this basis alone, the significance of this publication cannot be overemphasized. But, *Renkou lilun* is extraordinarily important on other grounds, as well.

In the course of the book, the authors of *Renkou lilun* keynoted parts of their exposition with the following words:

> A population plan is an important component of the unified national economic development plan ... the starting point for drafting the national economic development plan. In the absence of data from a population plan, there can be no way of establishing many planning items or even the entire national economic development plan itself. (pp. 46-47, below)

In other words, the book sets out to declare categorically that to solve the many gigantic problems facing China—agricultural production, industrial growth, provision of cultural, educational and health services, housing construction, etc.—is going to require a close partnership of the state with the science of demography.

Renkou lilun comprises the following eight chapters:

1. A Critique of Malthus' Principle of Population
2. The Basic Premises of the Marxist Theory of Population
3. The Problem of Population in Capitalist Society
4. The Law of Population in Socialist Society
5. The Control of Our Nation's Population Growth According to Plan
6. Population Plan
7. The Gradual Attainment of Universal Planned Reproduction (Family Planning)

---

*In June 1978, the Office was transferred to the Chinese People's University in Beijing (Peking), and it is now known as the Institute of Population (Theory) Research. Liu Zheng, the senior author of *Renkou lilun*, is the director of the Institute.

8. A Critique of Contemporary Bourgeois Population Theories and Policies

In the present volume, I have translated three chapters of the book. As chairperson of the Committee on China Study and Exchange of the Population Association of America, I felt that by this effort to circulate among Western demographers a recent work written by their professional colleagues in China, I might be able to help advance normalization of professional relations between them.

Specifically, I have translated Chapters 5, 6, and 7. The decision to limit my present effort to translating only three chapters, while dictated in part by other time-consuming duties, was based principally on my desire to maximize and accelerate communication and exchange. The three chapters selected, in my judgment, provide the most telling and timely details of China's attitudes toward and steps taken in the control of population growth. They also reveal a great deal of information that had not been published previously, systematically or otherwise.

Planned population growth: terms of reference

The most oft-quoted statement on the Chinese population question is Chairman Mao Zedong's pronouncement on September 16, 1949:

> It is a very good thing that China has a big population. Even if China's population multiplies many times, she is fully capable of finding a solution. . . . (In short) . . . revolution plus production can solve the problem of feeding the population. . . . Of all things in the world, people are the most precious. Under the leadership of the Communist Party, as long as there are people, every kind of miracle can be performed. (Mao, 1961: 453-454)

This pronouncement that people are the most precious of all things in the world would remain the leading premise of almost all subsequent statements on the Chinese population question. In various speeches before international audiences, Chinese officials have reaffirmed this principle in their descriptions of what China has sought to achieve in the area of population growth (Appendices D, E, and F). For example, speaking before the 1973 ECAFE meeting in Tokyo, Chi Lung stated,

> We hold that, of all things in the world, people are the most precious.

People are the decisive factor in the social productive forces. They are first of all producers and then consumers. (p. 90, below)

But he and others also described China's population policy in other terms: In Chi Lung's words,

Population increase in a planned way is China's established policy. We follow such a policy not because the question of "over-population" exists in China. In China, social production is carried out in a planned way and this requires that the population increase is planned, too. It is also necessary to have a planned population increase in order to promote the thorough emancipation of women, care for mothers and women and children and bring up and educate the younger generation well, and improve the people's health and bring about national prosperity. Such a policy conforms with the interests and aspirations of the broad masses. (p. 92, below)

At the seventeenth session of the United Nations Population Commission in November 1973, Yu Wang made an important elaboration:

. . . We do not approve of anarchy either in material production or in human reproduction. Man should control himself as well as nature. (p. 95)

Huang Shu-tse termed China's policy as "the planned regulation of the rate of population growth." (p. 104, below)

Clearly, China's population policy in the 1970s is predicated upon more numerous considerations than before. Some of the considerations (e.g., the protection of mothers, women and children, the bringing up of the younger generation, and the improvement of the people's health and national prosperity) are not new. These were the prominent ingredients of the policy of the 1956-57 period. What is strikingly new is the theme that human reproduction, like the production of goods and services in a planned economy, must not remain in a state of anarchy but be regulated according to plan.

So formulated, the policy of the 1970s seems to have been built on a foundation not blueprinted in Mao's 1949 pronouncement. In fact, not until recently has it been clearly established that Chairman Mao personally ever sanctioned fertility control. In the well-known "On the Correct Handling of Contradictions among the People," Mao Zedong stated on February 27, 1957, that

. . . we have a population of 600 million, that is an objective fact, and that it is an asset for us. Our large population is a good thing, but of

course it also involves certain difficulties. . .—this is a contradiction. . . .
(Mao, 1977: 407)

Reportedly, as shown in an advanced version of the speech in circulation in Warsaw, Poland, in June 1957, Mao also said that in view of the slow increase in grain production and of the many youths not being able to enter primary schools,

> . . . steps must therefore be taken to keep our population for a long time at a stable level, say, of 600 million. A wide campaign of explanation and proper help must be undertaken to achieve this aim. (*The New York Times*, June 13, 1957)

But this latter passage does not appear in any official translations of the speech. Thus, few direct quotations from Mao's writings emerged in the 1950s and 1960s that conveyed his direct blessings of family planning, although he presumably supported it from the late 1950s onward.

With the publication of Volume V of *Selected Works of Mao Tsetung* in March 1977, however, it can now be verified that Mao formally endorsed family planning in October 1957. In an address at the Enlarged Third Plenary Session of the Eighth Central Committee of the Chinese Communist Party, he said,

> In my opinion, China must depend on intensive cultivation to feed itself. One day China will become the world's number one high-yield country. . . . I think an average of three *mou* of land per person is more than enough and in future less than one *mou* will yield enough grain to feed one individual. Of course birth control will still be necessary, and I am not encouraging more births. . . . There should also be a ten-year program for family planning. However, it should not be promoted in the minority nationality areas or in sparsely populated regions. . . . [See Appendix I for an example of this policy in action.] As far as procreation is concerned, the human race has been in a state of total anarchy and has failed to exercise control. . . . (Appendix B, p. 88)

These words also constitute the terms of reference for China's planned population growth policy of the 1970s. The thrust of the various speeches by Chinese officials at recent international gatherings is also fully in keeping with them. Similarly, the authors of *Renkou lilun* have also adhered to them in their delineation of China's planned population growth. (Chapter 5, p. 42)

In the course of their exposition, however, the writers underscore China's regulation of population increase according to plan with more detailed theorization. Thus, in this volume, for the first time since the 1950s, China's evolving attitude toward the control of population growth is more fully depicted.

One noteworthy point is the linkage of planned population growth to the issue of accumulation and consumption (pp. 29-31). Previously, Mao Zedong had put forth his view of the question of how to achieve "a proper ratio between accumulation and consumption," but treated it in nondemographic terms (Appendix A). In *Renkou lilun* the issue of accumulation versus consumption is translocated to the demographic context. What emerges from this is, among other things, the observation that the planned control of population growth means more room for adjusting the ratio between accumulation and consumption and facilitates the expansion of productive accumulation, more construction in the area of material production, and the overall expansion of the national economy. Although this is in keeping with the assumptions of various demographic economic models in the population literature outside China, the timing of its *emphasis* is significant.

The other salient features of the volume are the authors' systematic descriptions of the organization and operations of China's population planning effort, of its objectives and the steps involved in its execution, and of the many formidable obstacles still to be overcome in the course of realizing the stated goal of lower population growth via family planning.

Family planning: Definition, model, and attainment

Family planning, as it is conventionally understood in the West, refers to the desire and decision of individual couples to limit and space childbirths according to personal circumstances. It is a matter of private concern, though the practice has received increasingly more governmental sanctions and support in recent decades.

In China, while the encouragement given to fertility limitation has been couched in terms of the protection of the health of women, mothers and children, etc., family planning is explicitly and visibly a public concern. As such, it is a component of the population planning of the state. The issue thus is far more than that of bearing fewer children according to personal circumstances. As stated in *Renkou lilun*,

> We have regularly had to calculate the ratios between population and the means of livelihood, food grain, and other industrial and agricultural

products. This is a requirement of a socialist planned economy. If there had been no such calculations, there would have been no basis for a planned economy. (pp. 42)

A population plan is a requirement connected with the drafting of a unified national economic development plan. (p. 46)

[Accordingly] childbearing is not only an individual and family matter, but also a major event that has a bearing on the scope and rate of increase of the population of the whole nation and on socialist revolution and socialist development. (pp. 46)

Stated in these terms, the dissemination of contraceptive knowledge and technology in China is much more a matter of family planning as such. As the authors put it,

This is to place childbearing in each and every household on the track of the nation's unified plan and to overcome the anarchy of reproduction so as to realize planned population growth. (p. 46)

Family planning that is based on personal circumstances and schedules necessarily no longer suffices. In its place, a definition of childbearing, notwithstanding its highly private nature—its timing, frequency, and spacing—emerges that is unambiguously collective in all important aspects. Controlled childbearing in the Chinese formulation thus comes to be predicated appropriately more upon couples' awareness and acceptance of its advantages in societal terms rather than merely in terms of its immediate beneficial effects on the health of women, mothers and children, on the nurture and education of the young, and on study and work. The latter advantages have long and repeatedly been stressed in Chinese population planning propaganda. The specification and inclusion of the former in demographic literature, as is exemplified in the present volume, clearly suggests that *population planning* rather than family planning as such is the order of the day.

Of course, population planning and family planning are inseparable in actuality. But the distinction is important. The making of a population plan and its implementation are very different from the planning of family size at the level of the individual couple. In aggregate terms, the number of births that individual couples separately plan to have in the light of their own personal circumstances probably is always larger than may be desirable in societal terms. The essence of the exhortation "to overcome the anarchy of reproduction" lies precisely in the need to resolve this contradiction. In other words, the number of individually planned births within a specified period of time must be brought down as close as possible to, if not made identical with, the number of births deemed appropriate for the maintenance and improvement of the societal well-being. The starting point for population planning thus is collective welfare; whereas family planning proceeds from a couple's assessment of their own situation. All this is reflected in the procedures of China's population planning that are detailed in Chapter 6 of *Renkou lilun*.

In human reproduction as in agricultural and industrial production in China, the basic mode of planning is the well-known democratic centralism. The various steps involved in this process, in agricultural production quotas, for example, are first established at the national level and channeled down to provinces, counties, communes, brigades, and teams. These are discussed at each level. Each lower level can make suggestions to the next higher level to modify the original quotas. The final plan is drawn up on the basis of this feedback, which is then transmitted to lower units for implementation.

In keeping with this three-step planning procedure, China's population plans are divided into national, regional, and grass-roots population plans. Policy initiative (i.e. the determination of the population total at the end of the planning period, the specification of the needed reduction in the rate of natural increase, etc.) begins at the top, policy input (in terms of major or minor modifications of the national population plan) from regional and grass-roots units transpires in the course of the top-to-bottom and bottom-to-top transmissions of the national plan, and policy implementation obtains in the grass-roots units at the end of the planning process. It is, however, difficult to answer the question of how much give-and-take there is in the formulation of China's national population plan. In all probability, what has been and is being implemented represents a *modus vivendi* in the matter of reducing population growth.

As previously indicated, the stated goal is to "strive to lower the annual rate of growth of China's population to less than 1 percent within three years." This would require a reduction in births that is probably not easy to attain within the specified time period. The authors of *Renkou lilun* appropriately devote a whole chapter to discussing the still formidable obstacles to be overcome in the course of spreading family planning practices in Chinese society, especially in the countryside. (Chapter 7)

Leaving the question of policy attainment aside for the moment, it must be noted that population planning in China is perhaps unique in the field of population control—peer influence is very much the principal component of its foundation. As one student of the Chinese population has described it: China's birthrate may be viewed as a manifestation of the collective will. (Ravenholt, 1979)

The group dynamics of China's population planning are described in the text (pp. 49-52 below) and consist of the following scenario: within the framework of the nationally formulated population plan and target, population plans of such grass-roots units as the rural people's communes, production brigades, urban street committees, residents' committees, government units, factories, shops and schools are drawn up to "eradicate the mess of current unplanned reproduction" among their members.

> Typically, the birthrate (is to) be brought down a few points from the previous year, perhaps from 25 to 22 per 1,000. Individuals (i.e., married couples of childbearing age) . . . then meet in their production team, residents group, or factory workshop to discuss how to meet such targets. Calculating the number of births which would yield the proposed birthrate, they proceed to allocate the births among themselves—deciding whose turn it is to have a child in the coming year. . . . In the group meeting, each individual or couple submits a personal five-year birth plan. The group then discusses and reviews the plans. After repeated discussions and consultations, they draw up a group birth plan, aggregating the individual plans of members. . . . All group birth plans are channeled upward where they are aggregated and used to draw up a master plan for the entire unit. The lowest level where a master plan is drawn up is the commune in the countryside and the neighborhood and factory in the city. . . . To draw up a master plan that will reduce the birthrate to a level suggested from the above, and at the same time accommodate individual wishes as best as possible, the higher and lower levels must consult together several times before a final plan is adopted. The final master plan is often posted on the wall in the unit's health clinic and is expected to be followed much in the same way the production plan of an industrial plan is followed. Those who have pledged not to have a child in a given plan year are expected to practice contraception. (Chen, 1976: 95-96)

However, it must also be emphasized that population planning involves far more than simple manipulation of peer influence in China's basic social units to which individuals belong by reason of work, study, or residence. Rather,

the formulation of a population plan is a serious political task and *is also planning work of a scientific nature.* (p. 51, *italics* added)

As is stated in the translation,

in formulating population plans, we must first clearly investigate current demographic circumstances, including total population, broken down by sex and age, the overall and age-specific birthrates and death rates by sex, and cases of marriages and births conforming to the *"wan, xi, shao"* model. (p. 51)

All this is "to provide a concrete basis for formulating population plans" and thereby to assure the realization of the plans. In the latter connection, the overall objective of planned population growth, i.e., lower rates of natural increase via planned reproduction, of course, has to be operationalized and made part of the popular language and consciousness. This entails a redefinition of reproductive norms in keeping with the goal of population growth according to plan. The *"wan, xi, shao"* model is a case in point. This model calls for late marriage (late childbearing)—*"wan,"* longer intervals between births (four years or longer)—*"xi,"* and small family size (two children at most)—*"shao."*

In the course of China's efforts to foster population growth according to plan and to attain the policy objectives, exhortations to limit fertility have undergone both subtle and substantive changes. At the start of the open campaigns in the 1950s, the emphasis was clearly much more specific insofar as late marriage was concerned. Though not directly related to fertility reduction, the disadvantages of early marriage were described in terms of early and frequent childbearing and its adverse effects on the health of women and the nurture of infants. A great deal of discussion was specifically focused on the suitable ages at which men and women should marry. In contrast, discussions of fertility limitation were much less specific and generally devoid of clear reference to the number and spacing of births within marriage. (Tien, 1973, ch. 6)

Late marriage remains the first and most visible component of China's policy of planned population growth. However, the specificity of fertility ideal has steadily and sharply increased since the early 1970s. For a while, exhortations were couched in terms of the Zhou Enlai model of "One is not too few, two is good, three is too many." Implicit in this model is the two-child family size ideal. The *"wan, xi, shao"* model thus represents the most comprehensive attempt to redefine reproductive norms in the continuing struggle to lower fertility in China.

Thus specified, the national population policy objectives can be more easily translated into terms that are meaningful and manageable at the level of individual couples. By the same token, as the authors of *Renkou lilun* also make clear, in the basic population planning units (i.e., rural people's communes, production brigades, urban street committees, etc.), the specifications of the *"wan, xi, shao"* model also constitute the criteria by which family planning work progress is evaluated. In fact, the *"wan, xi, shao"* model provides the guidelines for deciding whose turn it is to have a child in a population plan year. That is, couples who are recently married at relatively late age and/or who have had a child awhile back (e.g., four years ago) are given preferential consideration by their peers in the grass-roots units to which they belong.

Undoubtedly, as has been previously indicated, there remain numerous obstacles of major dimensions that must be overcome if China is to attain planned population growth at the rate of 1 percent per annum. Awareness of the existence of these obstacles is clearly registered in the authors' discussion of how to

> promote family planning "step by step until family planning gradually becomes universal," and to achieve "the complete realization of family planning in the future." (Chapter 7, p. 63)

Of particular interest here are the various specific measures for overcoming the still formidable barriers to the gradual attainment of universal planned reproduction. These make evident that ancient reproductive norms remain powerful, especially in the countryside where the majority of the population lives. The mobilization of both government cadres and the masses thus constitutes and is likely to continue as the leading task in planned population growth in China.

In this connection, and going beyond the translated text, the urgency of the task of lowering fertility is most vividly demonstrated by the fact that new measures are being implemented in Sichuan, China's most populous province. Designed to encourage one-child families, the measures include a monthly payment of 3.75 *yuan* to couples in the cities who have only one child and who promise not to have a second child until the first child is fourteen years old. In addition, urban couples are entitled to extra housing allocations as if they were a two-child family, and priority will be given to "single" children either in the admission to school or in the assignment of a job. In the villages, one-child couples will receive a monthly payment of an amount equal to three workdays until the child is fourteen years old. A single child also gets the same amount of food grain ration as an adult as well as 1.5 shares of plots for private use. Thus, the mobilization of the masses in fulfilling the country's population plan has shifted into high gear. The benefits of limited childbearing are spelled out in economic terms of both an immediate and a long-term character. Presumably, all this is to supplement, rather than supplant, the measures that have been extensively introduced throughout China to reduce the anarchy of reproduction via mass education and collective discussions and decision.

* * *

In keeping with China's decision to reform the Chinese language, all proper nouns in the Introduction and translations from *Renkou lilun* are rendered in the *pinyin* system of romanization. For example, Mao Tse-tung is now spelled Mao Zedong, and Jutung is now spelled Rudong. However, in sources and reprints that precede the change to *pinyin*, I have followed the original and let the Wade-Giles spelling stand.

REFERENCES

Chen, P. C. (1976) *Population and Health Policy in the People's Republic of China*, Washington, D.C.: Smithsonian Institution.

Frejka, Tomas (1976) "One-Fifth of Humanity," *People*, 3(3): 4-5.

Hua, Guofeng (1978) "Unite and Strive to Build a Modern Powerful Socialist Country," Report of the Government, the Fifth National People's Congress, First Session, Peking.

Mao, Zedong (1961) *Selected Works of Mao Tse-tung*, Peking: Foreign Languages Press, Vol. IV.

_____(1977) *Selected Works of Mao Tsetung*, Peking: Foreign Language Press, Vol. V.

People's Daily (Renmin ribao), July 9, 1978.

Ravenholt, Rei T. (1979) "China's Birth Rate: A Function of Collective Will," Paper presented at the 1979 annual meeting of the Population Association of America, Philadelphia.

The New York Times, June 13, 1957, and February 3, 1964.

Tien, H. Yuan (1973) *China's Population Struggle: Demographic Decisions of the People's Republic, 1949-1969*, Columbus, Ohio: The Ohio State University Press.

_____(1975) "Fertility Decline Via Marital Postponement in China," *Modern China*, *1*(4): 447-62.

Translations from
Renkou Lilun

der among mankind can be achieved. Chairman Hua has also deemed that a large population is one of the advantageous conditions in the course of developing our nation, within the present century, into a powerful socialist country fully modernized in agriculture, industry, defense, and science and technology.

But a large population also means difficulties. These difficulties are none other than the problems of food, employment, and education. Such difficulties, of course, are temporary problems of progress which can be totally resolved on the basis of the superior socialist system itself. Chairman Mao pointed out,

> Progress and at the same time difficulties—this is a contradiction. However, not only should all such contradictions be resolved, but they definitely can be. Our guiding principle is overall consideration and proper arrangement. Whatever the problem—whether it concerns food, natural calamities, employment, education, the intellectuals, the united front of all patriotic forces, the minority nationalities, or anything else—we must always proceed from the standpoint of overall consideration, which embraces the whole people, and must make the proper arrangement, after consultation with all the circles concerned, in the light of what is feasible at a particular time and place. (Mao, 1977: 407)

In their attack, Khrushchev and his traitorous clique said that the view that a large population is a good thing "reflects the traditional view of China's early feudal society that large families mean large enterprises as well as the Sino-centric notion that a large population is the pillar and sign of national wealth, which is in essence a chauvinistic notion" (*New Time*, 1974: No. 33: 23). This is malicious slander. Our statement that a large population is a good thing is based on the premise that "of all things in the world, people are the most precious." It has nothing in common with the so-called "feudal view of large families meaning large enterprises," "Sino-centric notion," or "essentially chauvinistic notion." As the whole world knows, having inherited the cassock and bowl of the old czars, the new czar has been plundering and expanding everywhere, attempting to establish an empire spanning Europe, Asia, Africa, and Latin America and to create global hegemony. In order to achieve worldwide hegemony, he must necessarily possess well-equipped, large, and aggressive armed forces. Precisely on account of this, Khrushchev and his traitorous clique today strenuously advocate population increase. Therefore, it is not surprising that Khrushchev and his traitorous clique have associated a large population with the chauvinism and hegemonism of large countries as well as related it to the attempt to become a global hegemonist and the center of the whole world. This is exactly a self-portrait of the expansionist design of Soviet socialist imperialism.

The Khrushchev traitorous clique has attacked in yet another way: in China since the beginning of the 1960s, the slogan "a large population is a good thing" has been supplanted by the slogan "a large population is a good thing and at the same time also a bad thing" (*Ibid.*). This is a shamefully fabricated rumor. In the past, in the present, and in the future our approach to a large population, like the treatment of any other problem, has always been and will be based on the insistence on the two-aspect perspective of Marxism in opposition to the uni-aspect perspective of metaphysics. Chairman Mao instructed us, "There will always be two aspects, even ten thousand years from now. Each age, whether the future or the present, has its own two aspects. . . . In short, there are two aspects to everything, not just one" (Mao, 1977: 303). We consider that a large population is a good thing; that is the chief aspect. But, we have never overlooked the other aspect that a large population can bring difficulties. As early as the 1950s, Chairman Mao clearly pointed out that a large population entails difficulties; at the same time, he indicated that a large population is a good thing. The rumors and slanders of the Khrushchev traitorous clique only serve to make evident their total betrayal of Marxism and Leninism, and to make clear that they have descended to a despicable and shameless level where, apart from spreading rumors and slanders, they cannot continue muddling through another day.

In the matter of handling a large population we must insist on "one divides into two." We must also insist on "one divides into two" in the matter of handling the high rate of natural increase. One is optimism, and two is control.

We firmly hold: the masses of people are the makers of history; of all things in the world, people are the most precious; the masses of people possess creative power of unlimited proportions; the ability of mankind to transform nature is boundless; the wealth of nature is inexhaustible and cannot be exhausted; and the future of mankind is infinitely bright. Engels said, "The productive forces under the control of mankind are unlimited. The application of capital, labor and science will raise the returns from land limitlessly." (Marx and Engels, 1956: 616)

Our country has already established a superior socialist system. This system has not only liberated the vast number of laboring people and the means of production, but also opened up Nature, which old China had no way of utilizing. Among our nation's huge population there is an extremely large reserve of socialist enthusiasm. We wholly believe that as long as we fully mobilize our nation's vast human numbers and organize them into undertaking work in all spheres and branches as well as tackling production more intensively and extensively, it will be possible for people to "initiate more and more undertakings for their own well-being" (Mao, 1977: 260). Today our nation uses less than 7 percent of the world's arable land to feed more than one-fifth of the world's population. "One day China will become the world's number one high-yield country," and "less than one *mou* (1/6 acre of land) will yield enough grain to feed one individual" (Mao, 1977: 486-7). Furthermore,

> In the days to come all kinds of enterprises undreamed of before will make their appearance and agricultural output will rise several times, a dozen times, perhaps scores of times, above the present level. The expansion of industry, communications and exchange will defy the imagination of past generations. It will be the same with science, culture, education and health work. (Mao, 1977: 268-269)

Therefore, in a nutshell, "even if the population increases many times, there remains a solution, and this solution is production" (Mao, 1969: 1400). Chairman Mao said, "We depend on intensive cultivation to feed ourselves, and even with a fairly large population we still have enough food." (Mao, 1977: 486)

That we maintain an optimistic outlook on the rate of population growth does not mean there is no need for control. We certainly must control the rate of population growth. This is a conclusion that we ourselves arrived at after we had mastered and applied the objective socialist law of planned population growth. We advocate planned population increase and are opposed to blind and unlimited population growth. The aims of our nation's efforts to control population growth in order to reduce the rate of increase according to plan are to bring into full play the advantages of a large population and to overcome its drawbacks as well as to give full play to people as the most precious asset. What are the reasons for doing this? The reasons are:

First, to do so serves to facilitate the complete emancipation of women and to bring into full play the role of women as producers.

In the final analysis, to bring into full play the advantages of our nation's large population is to maximize thoroughly the role of people as producers. In our country, women constitute one half of the population. Therefore, to maximize thoroughly the role of people as producers, one major task is to mobilize the broad masses of women to join in social production, transforming the great majority of women from consumers into producers. Chairman Mao pointed out, "Women form a great reserve of labor power in China. This reserve should be tapped in the struggle to build a great socialist country." (Mao, 1977: 269)

But our nation's women, particularly the broad masses of peasant women, have not now been able to shake themselves free from the burden of high birthrates and household chores. According to investigation, in some places, before extensive family planning was introduced, women of reproductive age had an average of six to seven children and could not participate in collective productive labor throughout the year. In this way, the great bulk of time in the women's life was taken up by pregnancies, childbirth, breastfeeding, and child care. They naturally could not become a decisive element in the productive force. Nor could women bring into full play their producer role.

In order to unearth this huge labor power reserve among our nation's broad masses of women, we must make it possible for them to shake off the unreasonable circumstances surrounding monotonous childbearing, childrearing, and tedious domestic chores. Thus, the planned control of the rate of population growth and its gradual decrease cannot but be a comparatively more effective and more realistic measure. The implementation of family planning to control the rate of population growth serves gradually to lower women's high rate of reproduction and to lighten their burden of childbearing and domestic chores, making it possible for them to leave home to join in societal production. A vast amount of factual data from various parts of the country have fully supported this. For example, in Nangong County, Hebei Province, because of extensive and deep-reaching implementation of planned reproduction in conjunction with the movement embodied in the slogan "In agriculture, learn from Dazhai," the rate of labor participation among women has increased to 90 percent from 60 percent in the past, and the proportion of women who participated in collective production has gone up by some 30 percent. In 1972, Nangong was still a county that consumed grain supplied by the state. By 1974, it became a county that produces surplus grain for the state granary. To cite another example, Rudong County, Jiangsu Province, is also a county where both "In agriculture, learn from Dazhai" and planned reproduction have progressed well. According to investigation, in the past, couples in the county had four to five children on the average. Now, the average is two, and the interval between births is always more than four years. The rate of labor participation among women increased from about 75 percent in 1970 to over 95 percent in 1976. In this county, women who have been liberated to participate in production number over 40,000 (*People's Daily*, July 6, 1977), exerting fully the function of "one-half of the sky" and contributing to the extension of the movement of "In agriculture, learn from Dazhai." Practice also proves that in units where women labor power is centralized, the adoption of planned reproduction and of reasonable arrangements for, and staggering of, women's turns to have children serves to avoid the adverse impact that simultaneous births among women have on the rate of labor participation and production expansion.

Furthermore, to control population growth according to plan and to reduce gradually women's high birthrates is also to enable women to participate in a positive way in politics and in the running of the nation, and to gain economic independence as well as real equality between men and women.

Second, to do so will also benefit the overall nurture of the new generation morally, intellectually, and physically as well as bring into full play the principle that people are the most precious asset.

Socialist society and communist society do not require blind and unlimited population growth, but call for the development of members of society in all spheres. Engels said,

> All of the following will be the most important results of the abolition of the system of private ownership: collectives made up of all societal members will make full use of their productive forces collectively and according to plan; the development of production will reach a scope wherein the needs of all members of society are met; class and class antagonism will be thoroughly eliminated. By means of the abolition of the old division of labor and the initiation of production education, rotation of work assignments, universal enjoyment of amenities created by all, and the merger of urban and rural areas, the development of members of society in all aspects will be attained. (Marx, 1972: 223-4)

Lenin also pointed out, we must "educate, train and foster persons of all-round development, that is, persons capable of all types of work" (Lenin, 1972: 205). Chairman Mao had a deep concern for the development of the new generation and pointed out time and again that we must "take good care of children," "must think more in the interest of our children and youth," and must change the circumstance of "adults simply [not bothering] themselves about their children" (Mao, 1977: 97). Chairman Mao also instructed that we must nurture children such that ". . . everyone [will] develop morally, intellectually and physically and become a worker with both socialist consciousness and culture." (Mao, 1977: 405)

If we continue to maintain the original high rate of fertility, and women give birth early, in short time intervals, and excessively, not only will all this adversely affect the health of children and mothers, it will also make it difficult for the family to devote greater energy to rearing and educating the next generation. Planned control of the rate of population growth, late marriage, and planned reproduction will enable women to reduce the number of births appropriately and to space them at suitably longer intervals. Not only is this conducive to the healthy growth of children, it also serves to allow the family to provide still more energy and time for children's growth. On the basis of such a reduction in the difficulties that a rapid population growth brings, the state will also be able to create still more numerous circumstances favorable to the nurture of the new generation in the moral, intellectual, and physical spheres.

Therefore, the planned control of population growth is more than the issue of bearing fewer children. It is a major issue that pertains to the health and prosperity of China's various nationalities as well as to the availability of successors to carry on the proletarian revolution. In other words, it is a major issue bearing on the future of mankind.

Third, in so doing, it will be conducive to rapid increase in labor productivity and to quicker realization of the four modernizations [i.e., agriculture, industry, national defense, and science and technology].

Rapid development of the national economy depends on an increase in the quantity of labor power and a steady rise in the level of labor productivity.

As regards the quantity of labor power, we are in an extraordinarily superior position. This is because (1) our nation's population is large, and our resources of labor power are very rich; (2) in our population, the proportion of youths is comparatively high, the supply of labor power will not be a problem in the future, and the requirements of high-speed development of the national economy can be fully met; and (3) following further rises in mechanization and automation, moreover, a portion of labor power will be saved. Chairman Hua pointed out that just in terms of agriculture alone,

> if the whole nation attains basic agricultural mechanization, and the level of mechanization in the main sectors of agriculture, forestry, husbandry, fishery, and subsidiary lines of production reaches 70 percent, then just from the standpoint of calculating [the impact of] mechanization in cultivation, irrigation, transportation, etc., it is equivalent to increasing the labor power in the nation's villages by more than 100 percent. (*Red Flag*, 1977, No. 1: 44)

Therefore, to expand the national economy rapidly, we should stress the utilization of workers equipped with new and more efficient technical tools, and the increase in labor productivity.

In our country at present labor productivity still is not high, the level of mechanization remains low, and each worker's technical equipment is of limited scope on the average. In order to enable our nation to catch up to and surpass, within a comparatively short period of time, the most advanced capitalist societies in agricultural production and in science and technology, it is imperative that labor productivity be quickly raised and that mechanization be widely adopted, and [see to it that] "in the technical field, machinery is used in all possible branches and places" (Mao, 1977: 203) in order to strive for the full attainment of the four modernizations within the present century.

The increase in the worker's technical equipment necessarily depends on the accumulation for production on the part of the state and of the collectives. But accumulation is always limited within a given period. Given that our nation's labor power is abundant, if a comparatively high rate of natural increase is to continue, it will adversely affect the elevation of the levels of technical equipment of the workers and of labor productivity. On the other hand, the planned control of population growth, which will result in the ability to control according to plan the increase in the number of persons reaching working age, will have a beneficial impact and serve to accelerate the rise in the level of technical equipment of the workers, realize the four modernizations, and raise labor productivity.

Fourth, to do so will speed up socialist construction and improve the people's livelihood.

Chairman Mao instructed us, "We want to carry on large-scale construction, but our country is still very poor—herein lies a contradiction" (Mao, 1977: 417). Our inheritance from old China is "one poor, two blank." During the last twenty-odd years since Liberation, we have made very large strides in national economic construction and cultural development. But, per capita output in agriculture and industry still is not high. In terms of Chairman Mao's stipulation that China "ought to make a greater contribution to humanity" (Mao, 1977: 331) and the lofty goals of the four modernizations that will serve to propel our national economy to the world's forefront, this circumstance of low per capita output means that we still have a very long distance to travel. This is an acute contradiction.

On each and every front we must strive to accelerate the resolution of this contradiction. And the front of planned reproduction is no exception. Given that our nation's human resources are already abundant, planned, gradual control of the rate of population increase will be conducive to resolving this contradiction.

The income of the citizens that is created each year in our country is ultimately spent in two ways: accumulation and consumption. Accumulation includes (1) productive accumulation that is invested in the expansion of further socialist production; (2) nonproductive accumulation that goes for nonproductive development, including culture, education, medicine and health; and (3) reserve funds that are used for defense and crop failures. The greater part of accumulation is productive accumulation to be used for expanding further production. The consumption component of the citizens' income is used to satisfy their material and cultural needs.

Under the condition of there being a fixed increase in the citizens' income, there will always be a contradiction between accumulation and consumption. When accumulation goes up, the consumption component will be less. Conversely, when consumption increases, the accumulation component will be smaller. There is a minimum to consumption, that is, to guarantee that the living standard of the total population (including newly added population) is not lower than that of the previous period. This is the minimum that must be set aside from the citizens' current income for consumption; this is also the maximal limit to accumulation. Accumulation also has a minimum, that is, to guarantee that the level of technical equipment of the total labor force (including newly increased labor power) is not lower than that of the previous period. This is the minimum that must be set aside from the citizens' current income for accumulation, and is also the maximal limit to consumption. The faster the citizens' income increases, the greater the absolute amount, which will provide still greater room for adjusting the proportions for accumulation and consumption, respectively. As we draw up an annual economic plan, we must appropriately arrange the ratio between accumulation and consumption in order to achieve the necessary balance between production and consumption needs. Chairman Mao said,

> (A) constant process of readjustment through state planning is needed to deal with the contradiction between production and the needs of society, which will long remain an objective reality. Every year our country draws up an economic plan in order to establish a proper ratio between accumulation and consumption and achieve an equilibrium between production and needs. (Mao, 1977: 395)

Accumulation chiefly reflects the fundamental and long-term interests of the collective and the individual. Consumption mainly reflects the current interest of the individual. Chairman Mao pointed out, "On the question of distribution, we must take the interests of the state, the collective and the individual into account" (Mao, 1977: 401). This is the guideline that we must follow in regulating the ratio between accumulation and consumption. Our way of doing this is: on the basis of production expansion and gradual improvement in the level of the people's material and cultural life, the ratio of accumulation is to be appropriately raised.

Given the present circumstances that our nation's population is large and the rate of natural increase is comparatively high, if the rate of population growth is lowered according to plan, it will clearly benefit the arrangement in the ratio between accumulation and consumption, helping to realize not only a gradual improvement in the people's life, but also an increase in accumulation. For example, if the rate of our nation's population growth gradually decreases from the annual average of 20 per 1000 to 10 per 1000 or even lower, it will be possible to save a certain amount of the consumption portion that otherwise would be spent for the newly increased population. This portion of consumption funds thus saved may be fully diverted to augment accumulation for the expansion of socialist production. Also, it may be totally used to improve the people's life, making it possible for the level of the people's life to rise more quickly. Or, a portion of it may be put into accumulation to be used for the expansion of socialist production, and the other portion used to improve the people's life. All in all, there will be a lot more room for adjusting the ratio between accumulation and consumption.

It must also be seen that because the population base has been expanding year after year, even if the rate of natural increase remains unchanged, the number of people annually added to the population will become larger and larger. On account of this, not only is an increase in consumption funds necessary, but an increase in the nonproductive portion of accumulation funds is also necessarily entailed. This is because, as population increases, it becomes necessary to make a corresponding increase in the basic investment in the areas of culture and education, health, public utilities, and housing construction. Under the condition of fixed accumulation funds, an enlargement of the nonproductive portion will affect the speed and scope of increase in productive accumulation. Therefore, the planned control of population growth will facilitate the expansion of productive accumulation, permit more construction in the area of material production, and accelerate the expansion of the national economy.

In many localities of our country, it has been shown that when the rate of population growth is lowered according to plan and in conjunction with the movement of "grasp the revolution, promote production," not only is there an increase in accumulation and a rise in agricultural and commodity productivity, there is also improvement in the people's life. Rudong County, Jiangsu Province, is such a case. In 1976, the rate of natural increase in the county dropped from 26.2 per 1000 in the past to 3.25 per 1000. In this way, as production continued to expand together with the simultaneous slowdown in population growth, the ratio between the county's population and food grain increased from 1:1.5 in 1956 to 1:2 in 1974. Every year there has been an increase in the amount of grain sold by the county to the state and in the county's collective grain reserve, and the lives of the commune members have also improved. In the six years from 1971 to 1976, the total agricultural and industrial output of the county went up 11.7 percent per year, food grain increased 5.1 percent, and the population grew at an annual average of 0.57 percent (*People's Daily*, July 6, 1977). In this way, population growth and the expansion of economic development have become still more responsive to one another. Accordingly, this has further facilitated reasonable arrangements in education, labor wages, and other affairs.

Moreover, the planned control of population growth can also move a step closer to perfecting the relations of socialist production. Stated in terms of the people's communes, as accumulation increases and production expands, the transition from production team ownership to production brigade ownership, from production brigade ownership to people's commune ownership, and then onward to ownership by the people as a whole, can be accelerated. Stated from the standpoint of the state, as accumulation increases, more enterprises owned by the people as a whole can be created to strengthen and expand the ratio and function of the system of ownership by all of the people in the two socialist types of public ownership, to give more support to the villages, and to reduce the differences between workers and peasants. Clearly, it is incorrect to view the control of the rate of population growth only as a matter of having fewer children, and not in terms of its effect on socialist construction and the perfection of the relations of socialist production.

From the above analysis, we have seen that the planned control of the rate of population growth and the maximization of the function of people complement one another. People as the most precious asset and the control of population growth are interconnected, though they are two different matters. To say that people are the most precious asset is to appreciate the place and function of people in social production, and to point out the fact that the masses are the makers of history. This appreciation is not based on the quantity of population or the speed of population increase. Regardless of the size of the population and also irrespective of faster or slower rates of increase, people are the most precious of all things; they are the decisive factor in the productive force, and the motive force in historical progress.

That we want to control the rate of population growth according to plan is precisely to bring into full play the function of people and the advantages of our nation's large population, as well as to overcome the defects of a large population. Facts have proven that our way of so managing [population affairs] has had beneficial effects on the complete emancipation of women, on the nurture and full development of the new generation, on the realization of the four modernizations, on the increase in labor productivity, on the amelioration of the people's life, on the elevation of the material and cultural level of the people, and on the further betterment of socialist relations of production during the transition to communism. Under our nation's concrete circumstances, the planned control of the rate of population growth is a Marxist decision and one major task in the furtherance of our nation's economic and cultural prosperity.

II. Regional differentiation in the planned adjustment of population growth

Our country's territory is vast, conditions vary from locality to locality, the distribution of the population is very imbalanced, and there are also very large differences in the stage of development and in the demographic circumstances among various nationalities. All this has been shaped by history. Therefore, planned population growth must take into account the concrete circumstances in different regions and among different nationalities and adopt different requirements and methods.

The Han people are our nation's principal nationality group. They constitute 94 percent of the national population and mostly live in areas of high population density. Chairman Mao instructed us that in densely populated Han areas, we should work "step by step until family planning gradually becomes universal" (Mao, 1977: 488). That is, on the basis of the voluntarism of the masses, we propagandize and popularize late marriage and fertility limitation and promote planned childbearing in order to gradually lower the birthrate in a planned way and in fulfillment of the demand "wan, xi, shao" in childbearing. By "wan" is meant the promotion of marriage at older ages. By "xi" is meant the practice of having children at longer intervals. By "shao" is meant the practice of having few children. We hold that the optimum age difference between parents and children is about thirty years, and that the best number of children is two. Actually, in the course of the implementation of family planning, individual couples who cannot have children should be given positive therapy.

To call on youths to adopt late marriage, to raise their age at marriage, is an important condition in the planned control of the rate of population growth. Late marriage means late parenthood, and creates the precondition for an increase in the age difference between parents and children. Late marriage is also an important component in the formulation of a population plan. But the benefit of late marriage is not at all limited to the control of the rate of population growth. More importantly, it has great significance for the maturation and full development of young people.

Youth is the crucial period for body growth, knowledge acquisition, and [life] foundation building, and it is also the period in life when one is most energetic and vigorous, most able to learn, most daring as well as full of drive. Therefore, young people should take full advantage of their time and strive to study Marxism-Leninism-Mao Zedong Thought, to study arts and science, to condition their bodies and to forge themselves into workers who attain full growth morally, intellectually, and physically, possessing culture and socialist consciousness, and they should not marry and have children early. Early marriage and early childbearing not only hinder study, but also are injurious to physical growth. Men and women, at age twenty and eighteen respectively, have just matured physically, but their various major organs such as the nervous system, organs, and bones have not fully developed. If they marry at such an age, it will do harm to their body. Chairman Mao instructed, "Young people between fourteen and twenty-five need to study and work, but as youth is the period of physical growth, much is imperiled if their health is neglected" (Mao, 1977: 96). Therefore, late marriage benefits young people, enabling them to become a morally, intellectually, and physically mature new generation.

For women, longer intervals between births, well-spaced childbearing, not only is conducive to the control of the rate of population growth, but more importantly, also is beneficial to the health of mother and child. Therefore, this appeal for longer intervals between births reflects the Party's and the state's concern for the people and for the protection of the health of women and infants.

When women have fewer children, not only is it beneficial to the nation's plan for population growth and to women's participation in production, work, and study, it also, more importantly, benefits the health and growth of the next generation. Therefore, the appeal for fewer children also concretely reflects the concern on the part of the Party and the state for the next generation.

To carry through the national appeal for "*wan, xi, shao*" in the light of concrete realities, positive steps must be taken to ensure that the rates of late marriage, fertility limitation, and planned reproduction reach the expected goals.

The rate of late marriage is the number of persons per 100 females or per 100 males marrying for the first time who conform to the age criteria for late marriage during a certain period of time. Naturally, it is difficult to reach a 100 percent late marriage rate because exceptions of various kinds and forms may be permitted. But, to the extent possible, the reduction of the various types of cases that violate the late marriage norm is the direction in which effort must be exerted. It is also one of the objective criteria by which to gauge achievement in family planning work. The rate of fertility limitation refers to the number of women per 100 married and fecund women of reproductive age who have actually adopted methods of fertility control within a certain period of time. We should popularize fertility limitation among married couples as fast and as much as possible, steadily raise the rate of fertility limitation, and accomplish planned reproduction. The rate of planned reproduction is the number of births per 100 total births within a certain period of time that conform to the requirements of the "*wan, xi, shao*" model. Compared with the rates of late marriage and fertility limitation, the rate of planned reproduction is of much greater importance. This is because it is a comprehensive index which serves as an overall indicator of whether or not age at marriage, interval between births, and birth parity are in line with the "*wan, xi, shao*" model. Accordingly, it is the chief index by which to assess planned reproduction. When the index is high, it indicates that few births are unplanned, that the number of births in keeping with the "*wan, xi, shao*" model is high, and that work in planned reproduction is comparatively advanced. Conversely, [when it is low] it indicates that unplanned births are numerous, few infants are born in accordance with the "*wan, xi, shao*" model, births are not being controlled, and work in planned reproduction is comparatively backward. Therefore, we must, in compliance with the Party's policy, adopt all measures to raise the rate of planned reproduction in order to control the birthrate and the rate of natural increase.

In densely populated Han areas, the promotionof late marriage and fertility limitation has already gained remarkable results, and the rate of natural increase has started to decline. For example, the rate of natural increase in Hebei Province reached as high as 20.25 per 1000 in 1970, but had declined to about 8.35 per 1000 in 1975. In Jiangsu Province, the rate of natural increase went up to 27.4 per 1000 in 1965, but dropped to 15.09 per 1000 in 1972 and further declined to 10.73 per 1000 in 1974. It declined another step to 10.02 per 1000 in 1976. (*People's Daily*, July 6, 1977)

Apart from the principal nationality, the Hans, our nation has fifty minority nationalities. The demographic circumstances of the minority nationalities have two special features of basic importance: (1) "The population of the minority nationalities in our country is small, but the area they inhabit is large" (Mao, 1977: 295). (2) Before Liberation the economic development of the minority nationalities was very backward, the livelihood of their laboring people was extremely poor, and their population either was unable to grow for a long time, or experienced an absolute decline, or was near extinction.

Using the principle of the total equality of nationalities based on Marxism and Leninism as the starting point, and in consideration of the special features of the demographic circumstances of the minority nationalities, appropriate measures should be adopted in the minority nationality areas to increase the growth of their populations. Chairman Mao said that in regard to fertility limitation, "it should not be promoted in the minority nationality areas or in sparsely populated regions" (Mao, 1977: 488). But in the case of those who have numerous children and who request fertility limitation, necessary instructions and assistance should be given. In so doing, it will facilitate the prosperity of the minority nationalities, strengthen the unity among all nationalities, and also be conducive to the opening up of the mountainous and border regions. All this will benefit socialist revolution and the advancement of socialist development.

Under the guidance of the correct nationality policy during the twenty-odd years since the establishment of the People's Republic, the economy of the minority nationality areas has exhibited visible progress. Medical therapy and health work have also advanced rapidly. Both the people's livelihood and their physical health have improved somewhat. The trend of population decline among minority nationalities has been thoroughly reversed, and there has emerged the heartening development of population growth.

In the Inner Mongolian Autonomous Region, the rampant diseases and population decline have disappeared. Since Liberation, the Mongolian population has increased year after year. By the first half of 1977, the population had grown to 1.3 times that at the beginning of Liberation. (*People's Daily*, July 15, 1977)

The Tibet Autonomous Region has developed quickly, and its economic appearance has undergone sky-turning and earth-shaking transformation. From the banks of Jinsha Jiang to the Ali Highlands, and from Yaluzagbujo Jiang to the Northern Tibetan Highlands, there have sprung some 200 medium and small enterprises which produce coal, hydroelectric power, agricultural implements, cement, leather, woolen fabric, paper, matches, etc. Accompanying the rapid and vigorous economic development has been a very significant growth of medical and health services. According to the Department of Gynecology and Obstetrics of the Tibet People's Hospital, the survival rate of infants has reached 98 percent. The population of Tibet as a whole has increased, and the rate of natural increase is now much higher than that of the era of predemocratic reforms.

The economy of the Xinjiang Uighur Autonomous Region has also greatly expanded. The total grain output during the five years 1966-1970 was 32.0 percent greater than that of the previous five years; the total output of cotton grew by 69.9 percent; and the value of total industrial production increased by 32.5 percent (Atlas Publishing Company, 1972). Health work has also experienced rapid expansion. Each and every county in the region has built a relatively well-equipped hospital, and the majority of the communes have health stations. Smallpox, which once ravaged the people's health, has long been eradicated. The population of the Uighur nationality has increased year after year. According to 1970 statistics, it has increased 42 percent since the beginning of Liberation. (*People's China*, 1972, No. 1: 85)

The population of the Oronchon nationality, which was nearly extinct before Liberation, has grown to over 2,700 persons. (*People's Daily*, October 1, 1973)

III. The intrinsic difference between our nation's control of population growth and old and Neo-Malthusianism

The basic antagonism between the Marxist and capitalist population theories is not over the issue of who favors population increase or who advocates population control, but lies in the question of who stands on what class position, upholds what viewpoint, serves which class, and has what aims. Marxist population theory not only is opposed to capitalist population theory, but is also opposed to the Malthusian theory of population control. It is erroneous to equate Marxist theory of the planned control of population growth with the old and Neo-Malthusian theories of population control.

Those who advocate population increase are not all Marxists. In feudal societies, there were many emperors, generals, and ministers who, on account of corvée and taxation, advocated population increase and adopted various measures to encourage population increase. But they and Marxists have nothing in common. At the time when capitalism was on the rise, some capitalist classical political economists advocated population increase. But they were not at all Marxists. Basing their views on capitalist exploitation of profit, capitalist classical political economists maintained that only labor capable of bringing profit is productive labor and that only the laboring population can bring wealth to the nation. The initial period of the capitalist expansion urgently needed a large quantity of labor power that could be utilized by capitalists at the latter's will. Therefore, they related population increase to increased supply of labor power for capital's exploitation, and so advocated population increase. William [Beatty?] was a population expansionist. He stated that people engaged in production are the wealth of the nation and that a small and sparse population means real poverty: a nation that has a population of 8 million is twice as rich as a nation of identical size in land that has only 4 million people. The chief representative of capitalist classical political economists, Adam Smith, was also a population expansionist. He asserted that production expansion and wealth accumulation necessarily increase demand for labor and hence require rapid population growth. Just as the demand for goods will affect the production of goods, the demand for labor will stimulate population increase, that is, the population increase that is needed by capital in its pursuit of profit.

The fascist chieftains Mussolini and Hitler and the Japanese militarists were all also typical population expansionists. Mussolini strongly advocated population multiplication. He cried out, "The power of population is, if not the chief determinant of a nation's political, economic, and moral power, then a preconditioning factor. . . . The destiny of a nation is closely affiliated with its population power." He also shouted, "Not only is the birthrate an indicator of the increase in the power of the fatherland, but it is also the basis on which to show and tell that a fascist nation is different from Europe's other nations. It is also proof of the vitality of a fascist nation and its immortal capability" (Mussolini, 1927). Starting from the aggressive and expansionist fascist ambitions, Mussolini also promulgated various measures encouraging population multiplication and preventing the birthrate from going down, such as encouragement of early marriage and large families, restrictions on emigration, and severe punishment for contraception. Hitler was even stronger in his advocacy of rapid population growth and external expansion. He scolded, "Not producing healthy children for the nation must be deemed an unpardonable act. On this matter, the state must serve as the guardian of its long-term interests. In this matter, an individual cannot have his own desire and selfish design, but must absolutely obey . . ." (Shirer, 1960: Ch. 1, Sc. 4). "Marriage should not be a goal in itself. It must serve a still greater aim: to protect the race and enable it to multiply and expand. This is the meaning of marriage, the duty of marriage" (*Ibid.*). In order to increase the population and to expand outwardly, Hitler called for an end to female employment, restrictions on enrolling women in institutions of higher learning, and restoration of women's "natural duty of reproduction." During these years Japanese fascists were likewise population expansionists. They vehemently opposed fertility limitation and advocated population multiplication and external expansion. The notorious Tanaka Gihito once wrote: "If our nation's influence in Manchuria and Mongolia is expanded by means of political measures, then it would follow that various requirements of a major power would be met. And, our annual population surplus of seven (or eight) hundred thousand would also find an outlet." (Wu, 1936: 259)

In order to enable American monopolistic financial interests to extract the greatest amount of profit, the contemporary American economist Kuznets espoused the view that foreign immigration or internal population increase should be induced in order to raise the relative ratio of young people in the population, thus guaranteeing adequate supply of labor power in the newly opened areas or branches where capital has streamed in as well as creating new purchasing power that facilitates the sale of commodities.

It can thus be seen that there are various kinds of people who have advocated population growth, to wit, feudal emperors and kings, capitalist classical economists, fascists and contemporary capitalist economists. They all start from the standpoint of upholding the interest of the exploiting class. We hold that under the socialist system, starting from the basic interest of the proletariat class and in keeping with the requirements of socialist development, it is necessary to achieve population growth according to plan. As for whether the increase is a little faster or a little slower, it is fixed on the basis of concrete circumstances. This differs fundamentally from the capitalist theory of population growth. If an equal sign is placed between the latter theory of population multiplication and that of Marxism, it becomes metaphysics, not class analysis.

On the question of the control of population growth, there are also substantive differences between Marxism and old and Neo-Malthusianism.

1. Differences in content

Our nation's control of population growth according to plan means planned and gradual control of the rate of population growth. It certainly does not mean no population growth or, even more so, it does not imply population reduction. It is only a matter of making the rate of population growth a little slower according to plan. Neo- and old Malthusianism advocate population limitation and population reduction.

2. Absolute differences in theoretical premises

Our nation's control of the rate of population growth according to plan is based on planned population growth in keeping with the socialist population law of human reproduction and built on the solid scientific foundation of historical materialism. Neo- and old

Malthusian theories of population control are built only on the so-called "law of diminishing returns from land," and on the subjective, arbitrary conclusion that the increase in the means of livelihood cannot keep up with population growth.

As stated previously, we are not worried about not having enough food to eat. That we want to control the rate of population growth is not at all because the increase in the means of livelihood cannot keep up with population growth. It is because we want to bring the function of people into full play, to build socialism at a still quicker pace, and to raise the level of the people's material and cultural life at a still faster speed. In a word, we are not concerned about "not having enough to eat" or being "unable to feed the population," but want to enable the people of the whole country to live still better, even more beautifully, and still more meaningfully.

We also routinely use data on population and the means of livelihood, particularly food grain. But this is a totally different matter from the population-food ratio based on fabricated data that Malthus proffered. We have regularly had to calculate the ratios between population and the means of livelihood, food grain, and other industrial and agricultural products. This is a requirement of a specialist planned economy. If there were no such calculations, there would have been no basis for a planned economy. Marx pointed out, "Bookkeeping is more important for capitalist production than for handicraft and peasants' decentralized agricultural production, and of even greater importance for socialized production than for capitalist production" (Marx and Engels, 1972: V: 152). Chairman Mao also repeatedly instructed us that to put into effect a planned socialist economy, economic calculations must be carried out. He said,

> Any socialist economic enterprise must make use of labor power and equipment conscientiously and as fully as possible and, in every way possible, improve labor organization and management and increase labor productivity. It must economize as much as possible labor power and materials, and practice labor competition and economic calculation in order to reduce production costs from year to year and to increase personal income and accumulation. (Mao, 1956: 768)

The so-called ratios of Neo- and old Malthusianism are altogether subjective fabrications. Neither the so-called "geometric ratio" nor the "arithmetic ratio" exists in real life. The reason that they spewed this nonsense was because they wanted to be at the service of the capitalists and to cover up the crimes of the capitalist system.

3. Basis differences in class aims

The aims of our nation's control of the rate of population growth are to bring into full play the strong points of our nation's large population, to overcome the weak points thereof, and to accelerate the development of socialist society in our nation. The aims of Neo- and old Malthusian agitation for population control are to deceive the laboring people, to divert them from their anticapitalist viewpoint, to defend the capitalist class, imperialism, and old and new colonialism, and to defend, at present, particularly the control, plunder and exploitation of the people of the world by the Soviet and American hegemonists.

We view scientific contraceptive methods as the means by which to attain planned reproduction and to make possible planned population growth. But Neo-Malthusians use contraception and fertility limitation as a pretext by which to promote reactionary social doctrines, deliberately distorting fertility limitation into the fundamental way of solving the population problem in order to absolve the capitalist system of its criminal responsibility. Among capitalist demographers, there are still those who at present confuse our nation's adoption of planned reproduction and promotion of scientific contraception with the Neo-Malthusian agitation for contraception and fertility limitation, as if the use of scientific contraceptive methods to realize fertility limitation *per se* is Malthusianism or a Malthusian tactic. This deliberately obliterates the basic antagonism between Marxism and Malthusianism because:

First, Marxism is never opposed to the adoption by mankind of necessary measures in the control of reproduction. Engels said that on the question of mankind's voluntary control of its own problems, "under any circumstances, in communist society people themselves are able to decide whether or not it is appropriate to adopt certain measures, when to use what methods as well as on the actual character of the methods." (Marx and Engels, 1971: XXXV: 145-6)

Second, our advocacy of scientific contraception and practice of planned reproduction are in conformity with the socialist public ownership of the means of production and reflective of the transition of mankind's reproduction from an inevitable regime to a liberal kingdom. That our people have voluntarily adopted scientific contraceptive methods and carried out planned reproduction reflects the fact that our people possess high political consciousness, are culturally sophisticated, and have learned to apply objective laws to voluntarily control mankind's reproductive capacity. This bears little similarity to Malthusianism, which advocates contraception and fertility limitation in order to reduce population and to obtain a balance between population and the means of livelihood.

Third, we advocate scientific contraception and espouse that the laboring people master scientific knowledge to gain the initiative in the matter of mankind's reproduction. This is an entirely different matter from that of Neo-Malthusian use of contraception to attempt to divert the laboring masses from their anti-exploitation struggle. On this, Lenin spoke very clearly:

> The freedom of medical propaganda and the protection of the basic democratic rights of men and women citizens are one thing. The social theory of Neo-Malthusianism is another. Awakened workers must always carry on a ruthless struggle to oppose the attempt to impose this reactionary, cowardly doctrine on the class that is in the contemporary world the most advanced, strongest, and most determined in carrying out great transformations. (Lenin, 1959: XIX: 224)

Simultaneously, Lenin also pointed out, "Of course, this in no way hinders our demand for unconditional abolition of all anti-abortion laws and also does not impede our support for the dissemination of medical writings on contraceptive methods, etc." (*Ibid.*)

Fourth, starting from concern for and protection of the people's health, we have, on the one hand, extensively expanded urban and rural health services and have made every effort to reduce the death rate. On the other hand, we have carried out planned reproduction and realized population growth according to plan. Malthusianism is completely the opposite. Starting from hostility toward mankind and a reactionary stand of animosity and hatred for the laboring people, it advocates the use of all methods to reduce population, proclaims poverty, hunger, and war to be the means of punishing people for their excessive multiplication; espouses the use of starvation to eliminate population; and blatantly declares war to be a powerful means of adjusting population numbers. The contemporary American Malthusianist William Vogt hates developing nations and peoples intensely. In his *Road of Survival*, he wrote that in developing nations, "of the many assets [. . .] perhaps the greatest asset is [their] high death rate" (Vogt, 1948: 186). Still others have said that the policy of spending a great deal of money by developing nations on public health and medical services is of doubtful wisdom because developments in these areas serve to reduce the death rate and thus inflate population growth.

Besides the above, Malthusians are basically racists and advocate the annihilation of so-called "inferior races." Hitler wanted to eliminate the Jews and other "inferior races." Soviet revisionist traitors are also racists. They vigorously advocate Pan-Russianism and, in dealing with various minority nationalities, have employed brutal measures such as suppression, amalgamation, and assimilation to exterminate them. Contrary to Malthusianism and racism, we advocate the total equality of all nationalities. In the minority nationalities regions, not only do we not carry on fertility limitation, but, on the contrary, we have adopted appropriate measures to boost population increases among minority nationalities and to further economic and cultural prosperity in the minority regions.

CHAPTER 6

Population Plans

I. The function, content, and types of population plans

In order to control the rate of population growth according to plan, it is imperative that quotas be established. This serves to define the aims and requirements of planned population growth within a fixed period of time and to provide the basis and direction for planned reproduction work. That is to say, in order to carry out planned population growth, we must work from our nation's existing demographic circumstances and, in accordance with the Party's policy, establish a population plan on the basis of investigation and research. A population plan is a requirement connected with the drafting of a unified national economic development plan. Its purpose is the realistic implementation of the Party's population policy. It is a powerful way of realizing mankind's need for self-control and to achieve planned growth.

Under our nation's socialist system, childbearing is not only an individual and family matter, but also a major event that has a bearing on the scope and rate of increase of the population of the whole nation and on socialist revolution and socialist development. Therefore it is necessary to establish a population plan that is based on the principle of coordination between state guidance and mass voluntarism. This is to place childbearing in each and every household on the track of the nation's unified plan and to overcome the anarchy of reproduction so as to realize planned population growth.

A population plan is an important component of the unified national economic development plan. Chairman Mao said, "In drawing up plans, handling affairs or thinking over problems, we must proceed from the fact that China has a population of 600 million, and we must never forget this fact" (Mao, 1977: 407). The unified national economic development plan includes such planning items as agricultural production, industrial production, transportation, capital construction, supply of materials, commerce, population, labor power, wages, labor productivity, culture, education and health, expansion of science and technology, costs, prices, and finances. A population plan is the starting point for drafting the national economic development plan. In the absence of data from a population plan, there can be no way of establishing many planning items or even the entire national economic development plan itself. In order to plan what and how much of consumer goods to produce; what construction in the cultural, educational and health fields to undertake; and how many square meters of housing space to build, data on the size of future population and its age-sex composition are required. The supply of such data depends on a population plan. Similarly, to determine the amount of labor power available during a planning period and the annual number of people who reach working age and who retire from the labor force and, furthermore, to determine how to allocate and utilize this resource of laboring power during the planning period also all require data on the total population and changes in the age-sex composition of the population. Such data must also be derived from a population plan. To draw up the long-term national economic development plan there is a particular need to grasp the direction of future population growth. That is to say, there is ever more need for a long-term population plan. Chairman Mao pointed out, "There should also be a ten-year program for family planning." (Mao, 1977: 488)

On the basis of the objective law of socialist planned population growth, our Party has formulated the policy of population growth according to plan. This is the Party's established policy. It embodies the fundamental interests of the proletariat, and also expresses the common wish of hundreds of millions of laboring people. The conscientious implementation of this population policy and the achievement of planned population growth thus require that a population plan be set. Only when both long-term and short-term population plans are established will the realization of a population policy be guaranteed. Our national population policy stipulates that population growth be according to plan, but how this growth should be attained during the next five or ten years and what rate of growth should be maintained cannot but be based on both a five-year population plan and a ten-year population plan. Moreover, our population policy stipulates that late marriage and fertility limitation be promoted in areas of high population density to control the birthrate according to plan, and that appropriate measures to facilitate population growth be adopted in minority nationality areas of sparse population. Thus, both the level at which the birthrate should be kept in areas of high population density and how the rate of population growth among minority nationalities should be adjusted must also depend on the provisions of the population plan. Without a population plan, it is impossible to carry out population policy; there is no other way to attain planned population growth. Therefore, to formulate a population plan that has scientific foundations is to obtain the initiative in the control of population growth and to attain the important link in planned population growth.

A population plan includes a series of targets. Among them the total population, the birthrate, and the rate of natural increase are the chief targets that constitute the basic content of a population plan. Therefore, in establishing a scientific population plan, the key is to determine correctly these three main targets. We now turn to a description of the basic content of each of these three targets.

1. Population total

The size of the total population is the basic target of a population plan, and is also the fundamental target of a national economic development plan. It is also "must" data in the determination of other planning items. A population plan is an important component of the national economic development plan, and its bearing on other planning items is centrally reflected in the size of the total population. The population total makes clear what the size of the national or regional population is during the planning period. Whether it is to fix the level of industrial and agricultural production, to determine the ratio between accumulation and consumption in the distribution of the national income, or to establish plans for expanding housing construction and cultural, educational and health services, we must proceed from the population total.

The determination of the population total during the planning period ordinarily pertains to the determination of the population total at the end of the planning period.

2. The rate of natural increase and the birthrate

The rate of natural increase is a dynamic target that indicates the rate of population growth during the planning period and is also the basic target of a population plan. Our nation's control of population growth according to plan is precisely a planned, gradual reduction in the rate of natural increase. The rate of natural increase is a function of the birth and death rates during the planning period. The higher the birthrate, the higher the rate of natural increase, the movement of both being in unison. The direction of change in the death rate is the opposite of that in the rate of natural increase. The higher the death rate, the lower the rate of natural increase. Expressed in terms of an equation:

$$\text{Natural increase} = \text{birthrate} - \text{death rate.}$$

Our nation's control of the rate of population growth will not, and absolutely should not, employ the method of increasing the death rate. This is incompatible with the character of the socialist system. The key to controlling the rate of population growth according to plan and to lowering the rate of natural increase is the practice of planned reproduction and the planned control of the birthrate.

Differentiated on the basis of the length of the planning period, population plans are of two types, short term and long term. Short-term population plans are annual population plans. Long-term population plans refer to five-year, ten-year, or even longer-term population plans. Those of ten-year or longer duration may also be called far-visioned population plans. Long-term population plans elucidate for short-term population plans the goals of the struggle and direction of effort, and they are the basis for drafting short-term population plans. Short-term population plans are the concrete guarantee for securing the goals of long-term population plans.

On the basis of the planning scope, population plans can also be divided into national, regional, or grass-roots population plans. Regional population plans refer to county, district, provincial, or autonomous region population plans as well as those of the municipalities directly under the central government. Grass-roots population plans pertain to population plans of the rural people's communes, production brigades, urban street committees, residents' committees, government units, factories, shops, and schools.

The formulation of the national population plan requires that the Party's population policy be adhered to consistently in order to reduce gradually the rate of population growth according to plan, and that it be closely aligned with the economic development plan to bring about an accord between population growth and economic growth.

Regional population plans are established in accordance with the goals of the national population plan, and must guarantee the fulfillment of planned quotas sent down by the state. This is to assure the realization of the goal of the control of population growth in the country. At the same time, regional population plans also provide leading regional departments with data on future population growth trends according to which regional production and construction enterprises' growth plans can be arranged and regional planned reproduction work can be improved.

The formulation of a grass-roots population plan proceeds directly from the concrete reproductive circumstances of every couple. The process of its complete formulation is also the process of boiling down the Party's population policy to concrete details, the process of propagandizing and promoting planned reproduction, and the process of mobilizing and educating the masses to integrate the interests of the nation with their own interests. Therefore, the formulation of grass-roots population plans provides the concrete guarantee for realizing our nation's planned population growth. Because the proportion of women of reproductive age varies in different grass-roots units, and because of differences in age composition, there is also diversity in reproductive circumstances. In units where the proportion of younger women of reproductive age is relatively high, the birthrate is commensurately higher; in units where the proportion of older women of reproductive age is high, the birthrate is commensurately lower. In formulating grass-roots population plans, full attention must be given to such actual circumstances.

II. The basic principles of population plan formulation

The formulation of a population plan is a serious political task and is also planning work of a scientific nature. In order for a population plan to become an organic component of the national economic development plan and a powerful tool for achieving planned population growth, we must proceed from reality and undertake sound investigation. We must achieve unity between the top and bottom branches and insist on the principle of democratic centralism [in the formulation of a population plan]. We must hold firm to the principle of aligning a population plan with economic planning and achieve unity between long-term and short-term population plans.

1. Proceeding from reality and undertaking sound investigation

In formulating population plans, we must uphold the reflectivism of materialism and be opposed to the experiencism of idealism; we must adhere to dialectics, oppose metaphysics, and carry out diligent investigation and research. Chairman Mao admonished, "You cannot resolve the problem, can you? Then, you had better investigate the current state of the problem and its history. When you have thoroughly investigated it, you will have found a way of resolving that problem" (Mao, 1964: 2). This is how other tasks are handled, and this is also how population plans are to be drawn up. We must proceed from the investigation of current demographic circumstances and estimates of the trends of future population developments.

Human reproduction is a continuous, unbroken process. Current demographic circumstances are the result of population changes during the past decades and also the basis for population developments in the years to come. Therefore, in formulating population plans, we must first clearly investigate current demographic circumstances, including the total population, broken down by sex and age, the overall and age-specific birthrates and death rates by sex, and cases of marriages and births conforming to the "*wan*, *xi*, *shao*" model. On the basis of these data, we shall estimate the trends of future population developments, discover laws, develop "a head for figures," and provide a concrete basis for formulating population plans.

2. Formulating population plans on the basis of unity between higher and lower branches and democratic centralism

The process of formulating population plans is precisely the process of carrying through and implementing the principle of democratic centralism. First, on the basis of investigation and research, the state puts forth its preliminary views on population developments. Then it mobilizes various regions and districts and various departments to discuss them thoroughly and to make suggestions for revisions. Finally, having gathered together the suggestions from the various quarters, the state draws up instructions on the control of population developments during the planning period and sets them up as the state planning tasks to be channeled down to various regions and districts for implementation. It can be seen that the formulation of the national population plan is the result of a great deal of work in which the great masses in various regions and districts and departments have participated and which has undergone top-to-bottom and bottom-to-top exchange. The principles of centralism based on a democratic foundation and of democracy under central guidance are embodied in this kind of unity between higher and lower branches.

In the formulation of a regional population plan, the principle of unity between the top and the bottom must also be adhered to. First, on the basis of the planning requirements sent down from the state, and in accordance with the estimated trends of the region's population developments and the extent of late marriage and planned reproduction work in the region, instructions on the region's population total, the rate of natural increase, and the birthrate are established and sent down to the grass-roots units. Grass-roots units broadly mobilize the masses to discuss the requirements of the higher levels, sum up the actual circumstances surrounding the number of women of reproductive age, the age composition and related matters, set up population plans of their own in accordance with the *"wan, xi, shao"* model, and then forward them to the higher levels. The regions integrate the plans of the grass-roots units and, on the basis of the requirements sent down by the state and taking into account the prospects for increasing the rates of late marriage and planned reproduction, establish population plans for their respective regions. Population plans established on the basis of this kind of exchange between the top and the bottom will place the planning requirements of the state and the actual circumstances at the grass-roots level in close harmony, not only conforming to the *"wan, xi, shao"* model, but also taking care of the matter of overall balance. Above all, owing to the mobilization of the cadres at various levels and the mobilization of the great masses, and having conducted much ideology and education work throughout the course of formulating population plans, population plans will be positive *and* reliable.

We must also see that the process of formulating population plans via the unity between higher and lower branches is precisely the process of setting into motion the initiatives of the center and the regions. It reflects the unified guidance of the center and also embodies the necessary independence of regional and grass-roots units.

*3. Coordinating the formulation of population plans
with plans for economic development, cultural development,
and expansion of service enterprises*

The economy of the nation is a unified whole. Among its various parts are internal links, interdependence, and mutual influence. As population plans constitute organic parts of the plan for national economic development, they have internal links to other planning items. Therefore, the formulation of population plans must be aligned with other planning items such as economic development plans and plans for expanding culture, education, health, science, and service enterprises.

The alignment of population plans and other planning items is achieved through the mutual harmony among planning targets. In concrete terms, it is realized through the mutual harmony between the planned targets for the rate of natural increase, etc., and the related targets for other planning items. Compared with the national population plan, however, the formulation of regional population plans has a special feature. That is, they must take into account mechanical movement in regional populations (i.e., in- and out-movement of people). The determination of this target is closely related to regional economic development. A region that, in accordance with the national requirements, undertakes large-scale capital construction during the planning period and greatly expands production will have to bring in a group of technical personnel and workers. Then, when it formulates its population plan, it must consider arranging in-migration and out-migration targets.

4. Achieving unity between long-term and short-term plans in the formulation of population plans

Because the population dynamic is a continuous process, the number of persons at present who can marry and have children is affected by the quantity of reproduction of the previous generation. This impact is not a short-term one, but continues for several decades. Similarly, the number and age-sex composition of the current total population will also affect future population developments for a long time to come. Furthermore, it requires ten or so years for infants to grow up to join the ranks of the laboring population. All this makes it clear that in the entire process of formulating a population plan, the formulation of a long-term population plan must be undertaken at the outset. A long-term population plan throws light on the trends of population developments within a comparatively long period of time. But it is not enough to formulate only a long-term population plan because it cannot accurately determine yearly population developments. For a population plan to be realistically meaningful in terms of guidance and direction, it is still necessary, on the basis of a long-term population plan, to formulate a short-term population plan to achieve unity between them. On the one hand, a short-term population plan is formulated in accordance with a long-term plan. At the same time, in the process of its formulation it can also furnish necessary supplements and revisions to a long-term plan because the implementation of a plan often uncovers new circumstances. The formulation of a short-term plan requires specificity and accuracy because it is a concrete plan for implementation, and the targets that it assigns to various regions and departments are national tasks that must be completed within the year. The connection between a long-term plan and a short-term plan is like the relationship between strategy and tactics. A long-term population plan is like a strategic move of overall significance, indicating the direction of future population developments over a comparatively long period of time. A short-term plan is like a tactical move of local import and a concrete step to realize the strategic goal. The formulation of population plans must obey the guiding principle of unity between long-term and short-term plans. Only then will it be possible for population developments to acquire an overall direction and have a concrete target.

III. The basic methods of formulating population plans

1. Preparing good population forecasts is the prerequisite for and foundation of population plan formulation

In order to establish a population plan that has sufficient scientific basis, it is necessary to carry out beforehand a scientific population forecast. Broadly speaking, population plan formulation itself includes the population forecast. It is possible to say that the population forecast is the foundation of population plan formulation and an organic part of the population plan. A population plan of broad scope includes work in two areas: (1) Grasping the trends of future population developments, and (2) establishing the planned targets of population developments, including the necessary measures designed to reach such targets.

The population forecast works from current demographic conditions, using scientific methods, to estimate and project the trends of future population developments. The more accurate the forecast, the more reliable the basis for formulating a population plan; the more realistic the plan, the more guarantee there is for its realization. Good work in population forecasting is the prerequisite for and foundation of a good population plan.

In terms of their order of sequence, the population forecast comes first, the population plan follows, and the latter must use the results of the former as its foundation. But the population forecast does not passively reflect the trends of spontaneous population increases in the future, but estimates the trends in the change in population developments in accordance with the *"wan, xi, shao"* model. Therefore, the population forecast already covers part of the population plan.

A population plan, however, is not a mechanical manipulation of the results of a forecast. The results of a population forecast only tell us how population developments will evolve under certain specified conditions. A population plan, according to the nation's demand for the control of the rate of population growth and the requirements of political and economic development during the planned period, must establish the population growth target and the measures needed to reach the planned target.

2. Basic content of the population forecast

The content of the population forecast is the content of the population plan because the population forecast serves as the foundation of the population plan. It includes three basic targets: the total population, the birthrate, and the rate of natural increase. The annual rate of natural increase sets the limit on the future's total population. Change in the rate of natural increase is principally determined by change in the birthrate, and estimates of the birthrate are, in turn, based on the current total population. These three targets are closely connected.

(i) Estimating Births

The key to estimating the birthrate lies in the estimate of births. The number of births is the function of two variables. The first variable is the number of women of reproductive age, i.e., the number of women who are above the minimum age for late marriage and capable of childbearing. Ordinarily speaking, the higher the number of women capable of having children, the higher the number of births. The second variable is the birthrate among women capable of childbearing, i.e., the annual number of births per 1000 women of reproductive age. Expressed in an equation,

$$\frac{\text{The birthrate of women}}{\text{of reproductive age}} = \frac{\text{Births}}{\text{Number of women of reproductive age}}$$

Suppose that in a certain locality in 1976 the number of women of reproductive age averages 10,000, and that there were 952 births; then the birthrate of women of reproductive age equals:

$$\frac{952}{10,000} = 95.2\%.$$

This is calculated on the basis of the total number of women of reproductive age. In actuality, women differing in age have different birthrates, and in some cases, the differentials are quite substantial. Furthermore, during the planning period, the proportion of women in each age group within the reproductive period also varies. Therefore, in order to still more accurately reflect women's ability to have children, it is best to calculate women's age-specific birthrates. Its equation is as follows:

$$\text{Age-specific rate}_x = \frac{\text{The number of live births among women aged } x}{\text{The number of women at age } x}.$$

Multiplying the age-specific birthrate by the estimated number of women in an age group, the product then is the expected number of births among women in the age group. Then, summing up the estimated number of births among all women of reproductive age, the total is the number of births during the planning period.

In the course of making actual estimates, the number of women of reproductive age is obtained by means of the age-specific survival method. On the basis of the number of persons in each age-group in the current year, the age-specific survival method predicts the number of persons in every age-group in the coming year, the year after that, as well as the final year specified in the demand for population estimates. For example, those who are twenty-five years old this year, will be twenty-six next year and twenty-seven the year after next. If we have the number of people aged twenty-five this year and take into account the death rate, we will be able to estimate the number of persons aged twenty-six next year, and the number of persons aged twenty-seven the year after next. Surveying persons in each age group from year to year, it will be possible to fix the number of women in each age group in any year specified in the demand for estimates.

In the course of making actual estimates, use is made of two kinds of birthrates. These are the actual birthrate and the model birthrate. The actual birthrate is the number of children ever born per 1000 women. The merit in using the actual birthrate to establish the number of births during the planning period is that its simplicity is suited to making rough calculations in the drafting of a population plan. Its defect is that it does not consider possible changes in the birthrate owing to the promotion of late marriage and planned reproduction. Therefore, this approach is not appropriate for making long-term estimates.

If all women of reproductive age should marry and have children in accordance with the *"wan, xi, shao"* model, the birthrate calculated on this basis would be the model birthrate. On the basis of the model birthrate and the number of women of reproductive age in the planning period, it is possible to establish the number of births during the planning period. The merit of this method is that it reflects the level of the birthrate after the realization of the *"wan, xi, shao"* model. But its flaw is that it does not allow for the impact of births outside the plan as well as for the fact that a portion of women have already married early and completed their childbearing early. Therefore, the result of using this method for making a forecast will also be somewhat at variance with reality.

(ii) Estimating Deaths

The second variable determining population increase or decrease is the number of deaths. In estimating the number of deaths, one approach is by means of the crude death rate, and the other is on the basis of age-specific death rates. In the case of the former, the equation is as follows:

$$\text{Number of deaths in the forecast year} = \text{Estimated population of the forecast year} \times \text{the crude death rate}$$

$$\left(\text{Crude death rate} = \frac{\text{Number of deaths}}{\text{Annual average population}}\right).$$

Use of the crude death rate to estimate the number of deaths requires only a minimal amount of information, and the method is convenient. If the period for which the estimate is made is relatively short, it is appropriate to use this method because the change in the current death rate is not large.

If the period for which the estimate is made is long, consideration must be given to differences in the age-specific death rates (for example, the infant mortality rate and the mortality rate among older persons are comparatively high, and youths and adults have lower death rates). Furthermore, it is also necessary to consider the fact that the proportion of persons in each age group in the total population may also change during a comparatively long period of time. Under these circumstances, even if the age-specific death rates remain constant, the crude death rate may nevertheless change. Therefore, to draw up a long-term population plan, it is better to use age-specific rates to estimate the impact (on the crude death rate) of change in the age composition of the population. Using this method to estimate the number of deaths involves four steps: it requires (1) the determination of the total population and population by age during the planning period; (2) the determination of age-specific death rates; (3) the multiplication of the number of persons in each age group by the corresponding age-specific rate to obtain the estimated number of deaths in each and all age groups; and (4) the addition of the number of deaths in each age group. The result is then the total estimated number of deaths.

(iii) Estimating Population Total

The increase or decline in the total population is due to two facts: (1) Natural change, i.e., changes in births and deaths, and (2) mechanical change, i.e., change in in-migration and out-migration. The effects of these two factors on population growth differ in character. Natural change in population is the main variable affecting population growth because in the context of the whole country the number of people who move in and out is minute compared with the nation's total population. In terms of different regions, mechanical change ordinarily affects population growth only in a small way. Only in newly built industrial and mining areas and cities is the effect of in-migration and out-migration comparatively large. Therefore, population forecasting is chiefly forecasting natural change.

Determination of the total population is based on the population at the beginning of the forecast period, taking into account births and deaths during the period. The equation is:

Population at the end of the forecast year = Population at the beginning of the forecast year + estimated births − estimated deaths.

Population at the beginning of the forecast year is obtained from statistics of the reporting year, or the estimate of population for the end of last year. Basic methods for estimating births and deaths have been described above.

(iv) Estimating the Rate of Natural Increase

To estimate the rate of natural increase, it is first necessary to ascertain the net population increase. Net population increase is the difference between births and deaths. The ratio between the net population increase and the average population is the rate of natural increase:

$$\frac{\text{Net population increase in forecast year}}{\text{Average population of forecast year}} = \text{Estimated rate of natural increase.}$$

The estimated rate of natural increase may also be obtained by taking the difference between the estimated birthrate and the estimated death rate.

3. Establishing population plan targets

The figures obtained through the population forecast are the important basis on which to draft a population plan, but they must be adjusted before they can serve as planned targets.

(i) Adjustments in Births

Regardless of whether projected births are estimated from the actual birthrate or the model birth rate, they are ordinarily at variance with the real circumstances. Therefore, only by way of adjustment can they be established as planned targets.

The number of births estimated on the basis of the actual birthrates includes births not in conformity with the "*wan, xi, shao*" model. Following deeper penetration of planned reproduction work, the rate of planned births, i.e., the ratio of births conforming to the "*wan, xi, shao*" model, will be gradually raised. Therefore, it is necessary to adjust the original estimated births in the light of the possible increase in the rate of planned births.

On the one hand, the number of births estimated on the basis of the model birthrate does not include the incidence of "early, close, numerous" births. On the other hand, it figures in the volume of births that occurred to women of reproductive age who have married and had children early. Therefore, to make the number of births specified in a population plan correspond to reality, it is necessary to take into account the effect of the former and to eliminate the effect of the latter. The number of births obtained in this way can then be used as the basis for a population plan.

(ii) Adjusting Population Totals According to Mechanical Change

When establishing the total population in the course of drafting a regional population plan, not only should the projection be based on natural change, but it must also take into account the shift in population numbers that may possibly be caused by mechanical change. Mechanical change ordinarily is closely related to the economic development plan. For example, a great deal of labor power must be transferred into newly created industrial bases. In some sparsely populated areas, a quantity of population is frequently introduced according to plan. Educated youths going up to the mountains or down to the villages, state recruitment of workers, etc., can also induce mechanical change. In order to ascertain the future population total, it is necessary to grasp the figures on possible mechanical population change. For this reason, it is necessary to keep in close touch with related departments to obtain information in order that adjustments may be made in the total population.

(iii) Leveling Peaks in Reproduction and Adjusting Population Growth According to Plan

In order to enable population to grow according to plan, not only is it necessary to eradicate the chaos of current unplanned reproduction, but it is also necessary to neutralize the effect of the historic condition of reproductive anarchy on future population developments. In the past, because of anarchic reproduction, reproductive peaks occurred. Persons born in peak years will successively reach, after a certain period, marriageable and reproductive age. Even if they marry and have children in total conformity with the *"wan, xi, shao"* model, there will still be peaks in the birthrate. Therefore, in actual projections, it often happens that even though the *"wan, xi, shao"* model is adhered to, the rate of natural increase does not go down year after year, but rises in some years.

The appearance of reproductive peaks necessarily causes unevenness in the annual number of births and often adversely affects national economic development. For example, the number of pupils entering school each year is determined by the number of births that occurred during the previous several years. When births occur unevenly, the variation in the number of pupils can be considerable, thereby resulting in the abnormal phenomenon that at times schools are crowded and at other times have plenty of room. This causes difficulties for the state in the regional arrangements for education. To ensure that population will sustain even growth according to plan, it is necessary to bring into play the greatest subjective initiative and to make every effort to achieve good results in realignment work and in leveling reproductive peaks.

Finally, it is necessary to institute periodic checks on the state of implementation. If problems are discovered in the plan and there are incorrect procedures, the plan should be revised immediately.

In inspecting the state of implementation, close attention should be paid to whether or not targets specified in the plan allow for differential treatment in keeping with concrete circumstances at the grass-roots level. In some grass-roots units, young people are many, and the proportion of women of reproductive age is high. The targets sent down should provide for differential treatment. If in the course of inspecting the state of implementation these phenomena are encountered, they should be corrected in good time and targets should be readjusted in order to facilitate the realization of the Party's policy.

In inspecting the state of implementation, we must grasp the key links and the weak links. In areas of high population density, the base population is large, and a 1 percent increase in population means an absolute increase that may equal or actually be greater than a population increase of 2 or 3 percent in other areas. Here, close inspection of the implementation of the plans in these areas should be undertaken and they should not be allowed to exceed the targets. Some areas have not energetically implemented the Party's policy for a long period of time. Thus, it will be necessary, following the establishment of population plans in such areas, to organize and frequently inspect the state of implementation of the plans, to discover and solve problems immediately, and to take steps to guarantee the realization of the plans.

CHAPTER 7

The Gradual Attainment of Universal Planned Reproduction

I. Planned reproduction is a profound revolution in the realm of the superstructure

In order to carry out the population policy established by the Party and the state, it is necessary to promote family planning "step by step until family planning gradually becomes universal," and to achieve "the complete realization of family planning in the future" (Mao, 1977: 488). In order to attain the complete realization of family planning, however, the souls of the people must be touched. Therefore, it cannot but be a profound revolution in the realm of the superstructure.

Viewpoints on marriage and reproduction are organic components of the superstructure and are dominated by the thought of the ruling class. Engels said,

> In every age, the thought of the ruling class is always the dominant thought. That is to say, the class that controls the material power in society controls at the same time the spiritual power. The class that controls the means of production controls the means of spiritual life simultaneously. Therefore, the thought of those who possess no means of spiritual life is ordinarily controlled by the ruling class. (Marx and Engels, 1960: III: 52)

For a few thousand years, the dominant thought in our nation has been the doctrine of Confucius and Mencius. After Liberation, and following socialist revolution on the political, economic and ideological fronts, although the doctrine of Confucius and Mencius has been criticized, its remnant poison has not been fully purged. Chairman Mao said, "Remnant old ideas reflecting the old system invariably persist in people's minds for a long time, and they do not easily give way." (Mao, 1977: 260)

To practice family planning, therefore, we must thoroughly expose and criticize the doctrine of Confucius and Mencius as well as thoroughly expose and criticize the thoughts of all exploiting classes and purge their poisonous residues. This is an important task in the realm of marriage and childbearing in which we employ Marxism to defeat the ideology of the exploiting classes.

At present, we should concentrate on the exposure and criticism of such reactionary notions as "fatalism," "males are exalted, females are demeaned," "begetting a son early," and "the more sons the more blessings."

"Fatalism" [*tianming lun*] is a main pillar of the doctrine of Confucius and Mencius. For a few thousand years, the ruling class of feudal society unceasingly promoted the notion of "life and death are predestined; wealth and status rest with heaven" to buttress their reactionary rule. According to their way of thinking everything depends on heaven and follows destiny. Marriage and childbearing are no exception. Whether a person is rich or poor, marries or does not marry, has children or not, has many or few children, etc., is all predestined. That the exploiters' chests are full of gold and silver, meats and wine go spoiled, and the laborers are destitute and die by the roadside is "predestination in life." That landlords take three wives and four concubines and lead a decadent, promiscuous and shameless life, but peasants cannot afford to find a wife is "predestination in life." That a rich woman bears one child and one survives, bears two and the pair lives, but poor persons have a bunch and bury the lot is also "predestination in life." How absurd all this is!

What is "predestination in life," and what is "heaven decides"? In the final analysis, it is nothing but what the exploitative system decides. "Heaven decides" is just another name for it. After Liberation, we overthrew the system of exploitation and thereby eliminated the various strange phenomena produced by it. Now, in China's vast land of 9.6 million square kilometers, who can still see the phenomenon of "inside red gates, wine and meat rot, while along the roadside lie skeletons of persons dead from exposure"? Who can still witness the miserable scene of great numbers of infants dying prematurely? Such phenomena are gone, and no one can see them. The masses say, "We do not believe in fate, but in revolution." This is the scientific conclusion of revolutionary practice and an unbreakable axiom.

Actually, human reproduction is not mysterious and incomprehensible. It is subject only to the laws of physiology and society. If we can only grasp the laws of physiology and society, we can become the masters of reproduction. In the past, the exploiting class took advantage of the people's ignorance of the laws of physiology and society and spread "fatalism," the aim of which was to absolve the exploiting system of its criminal responsibility. Today, we want to practice family planning, and we must simultaneously acquire knowledge of physiology and society and thoroughly expose and criticize the reactionary view of "heaven decides" in order to sweep away obstacles to the acceptance of family planning.

"Males are exalted, females are demeaned" is an important dimension of the doctrine of Confucius and Mencius. As expressed in marriage, it meant that men took a wife, that the wife obeyed the husband, and that the wife was a slave to the husband and the household as well as being a breeding machine. As reflected in childbearing, it meant that boys were valued more than girls. On account of the fact that ideology falls behind reality, the minds of some people today are still blinded, to a degree, by thinking of this sort. The kind of blind chase after many boys early in life is precisely the expression of this kind of thinking. And this kind of blind chase after many boys early in life is a major ideological barrier to the wide and deep dissemination of late marriage and family planning. Therefore, penetrating analysis and criticism of "males are exalted, females are demeaned" must be undertaken.

"Males are exalted, females are demeaned" is not something that dates from antiquity and never dies, as the exploiting class declared it to be. It was merely the product of a certain social, political, and economic system and is a historical phenomenon. As it was produced under certain historical conditions, it must be eradicated under certain other historical conditions.

Primitive communism remained in existence for a long time during the stage of matriarchal communes. Because of the commune's ownership of the means of production, and on account of its level of technology, the role of women in production was no less than that of men or was even more important than that of men. The marriage system at the time was that of group marriage. Tribes were formed on matriarchal lineage. Members of a tribe frequently elected somewhat older and more able women as tribal chiefs. As the system of group marriage gradually underwent transition to the conjugal marriage system of one man and one woman, it still remained that men were married to women and went to live in the latter's abode. At that time, not only did women enjoy an equal place with men, "they also occupied a position of high respect." (Marx and Engels, 1972: IV: 43)

Later, as the productive forces expanded, especially as agriculture and animal husbandry expanded, a fundamental change took place in the economic position of men and women. In agriculture and animal husbandry, men came to assume responsibility for such main production laboring tasks as felling trees, clearing land, plowing, shepherding, feeding livestock, etc. Women's labor increasingly dropped to second place. Men came to control the means of production and the power to distribute the means of livelihood. This cleared the way for the birth of the concept "males are exalted, females are demeaned." The appearance of the system of private ownership and the emergence of classes were the origin of the concept "males are exalted, females are demeaned."

Following the transition from primitive communes to the system of slavery, the enslavement of women by men also finally became established. Engels wrote, "The appearance in history of the earliest class antagonism occurred at the same time as the growth of antagonism between husband and wife under the system of monogamy. And the earliest class oppression occurred at the same time as the enslavement of women in the hands of men." (*Ibid.*: 61)

In our slave society, the slave-owning class established a system of rule in which the class system was patrilineal. The official titles and property of male slave-owners could be inherited only by male offspring. Female offspring had no inheritance rights. The status of women was also fixed on the basis of the husband's position. In order to maintain the system of rule centered on the patrilineal class system and to prevent the political and economic privileges of the slave-owning class from falling into the hands of outsiders, "males are exalted, females are demeaned" thereupon became the thought form of the slave-owning class, i.e., the dominant thought form in society.

When slave society advanced to the Spring and Autumn period [772-481 B.C.], because of frequent slave uprisings, the newly risen landlord class emerged, and the rule of the slave-owning class completely disintegrated. At that time, Confucius sprang forth and stubbornly supported the slave system, openly espousing the nonsense that "of all people, women and servants are the most difficult to deal with," and recklessly publicizing the notion of "males are exalted, females are demeaned." Later, Confucius' disciple Mencius related "males are exalted, females are demeaned" to childbearing and put forth the idea "of the three unfilial acts, the worst is to have no son," i.e., the absence of male offspring is the same as having no heir and constitutes the most unfilial act. Following the publicity of all this in the hands of the feudal ruling class of the succeeding dynasties, this reactionary saying of Mencius became the golden rule of "males are exalted, females are demeaned." Failure of women to bear a boy became a major crime, even to the point that it became a "reason" for the husband to jettison his wife.

In the Western Han [206 B.C.-24 A.D.] Dong Zhongshu proclaimed, "Banish the hundred schools of thought, respect only Confucian books." The way of Confucius and Mencius ascended to the position of being the dominant ideology in society. Dong Zhongshu advanced the so-called "Three Bonds," that is, "minister follows prince," "son follows father," and "wife follows husband," and thus further elevated the notion of "males are exalted, females are demeaned" to the position of a "principle" in the reactionary rule of the feudal landlord class. Thereafter, "males are exalted, females are demeaned" also became the spiritual pillar used by our country's feudal ruling class to prop up and consolidate their reactionary rule as well as the ideological tool used to oppress and enslave the masses of women.

Today, our nation has basically eliminated the system of private ownership and established the system of public ownership, and it has been liberated from the enslavement of the exploiting system. But, this, *per se*, is not enough. A further step must be taken toward liberation from the spiritual enslavement of the exploiting class. Otherwise, nothing can be said about complete liberation. We certainly must thoroughly criticize the notion of "males are exalted, females are demeaned," purge the residual poison, and embrace the ideas of the equality of the sexes and the equal worth of the birth of boys and girls.

"Begetting a son early" and "the more sons the more blessings" by means of "having several sons in succession" were also an important part of the way of Confucius and Mencius. "Begetting a son early" meant that the ruling class, in the interest of its rule, espoused early marriage and bearing a son early in order to perpetuate its power to rule, oppress, and exploit the laboring people. The ruling class imposed such viewpoints regarding marriage and childbearing on the laboring people to control and contort their thought. Confucius once said that men's "sperm flows at the age of six plus ten" and that women "become transformed at the age of four plus ten," and thus preached that it was possible for men and women to marry and have children at sixteen and fourteen, respectively. The ruling class of the succeeding dynasties never paid attention to the harm to the race that early marriage brings, and strongly publicized early marriage in order to increase still more laboring power for exploitation and still more numerous soldiers to strengthen their reactionary rule. In some instances, feudal dynasties went so far as to promulgate the written rule that when women were not married after fifteen years of age, they would be subject to heavy tax or forced to marry. Mencius once said, "If there were no rustic people, there would be none to support those of superior ranks." This quotation is the best example of why he publicized the notion of "begetting a son early" among the laboring people.

In terms of birth spacing, Confucius and Mencius espoused the notion of "having several sons in succession" and treated women simply as breeding machines. As far as the reactionary ruling class was concerned, the aim of "having several sons in succession" was to perpetuate their power generation after generation and to consolidate and expand their ruling position. From the standpoint of the laboring people, under the cruel oppression and exploitation of the exploiting class, "more sons" and "more miseries" are synonymous, as are "more blessings" and "more suffering."

Though the way of Confucius and Mencius still has influence in our country, its market has become smaller and smaller. Its complete extinction is predestined. The masses of women put it tellingly:

> In the old society, we were exploited, oppressed, and led a hard life. Knowing not the scientific contraceptive methods, we blindly reproduced, bearing many children and burying also many children. What suffering we sustained! In the new society, the laboring people are the masters. The state promotes family planning, of which the advantages for women and children and for the country are beyond count. This is not because our fate was unlucky in the old society and turned for the better

in the new society, but because the society has changed. We do not believe in fate, but in revolution. What Confucius said about predestination in life and death is all people-fooling nonsense.

But, we should not think that by criticizing a few times, the problem would then be solved. The way of Confucius and Mencius has, after all, pervaded our nation for several thousand years. The wide scope of its influence and the depth of its evil have few parallels. That we want to criticize the way of Confucius and Mencius and purge its remnant poison cannot but involve thousands of families and tens of thousands of households as well as touch the souls of hundreds of millions of people. We must fully fathom the formidable, complex, and long-term character of the struggle in the ideological sphere. The belief that a few rounds of propaganda and a few rounds of criticism can solve the problem is not realistic.

Criticizing the way of Confucius and Mencius and overcoming the old ideas in the areas of marriage and childbearing are, under most circumstances, the problems of internal contradictions among the people. The resolution of internal contradictions among the people depends on persuasive education and ideology work, and on the masses' own efforts to educate themselves. Chairman Mao instructed, "Family planning requires open education, which means airing views freely and holding great debates." (Mao, 1977: 488)

Simultaneous with the destruction of the way of Confucius and Mencius, there must be sweeping propagandizing of the viewpoints of the proletariat. Propagandize that human beings must control themselves and carry out planned growth, that as times have changed, men and women have become equal, and that for the sake of revolution one should marry late and practice family planning.

Not only must there be propaganda, there must also be measures adopted to stimulate the social revolution of "destroying the old, establishing the new" and "changing existing habits and customs" in the areas of marriage and childbearing.

First, insistence must be placed on the principle of distribution according to his or her work. Chairman Mao instructed, "In production, men and women must receive equal pay for equal work" (Mao, 1977: 263). On the basis of this principle, we get rid of the unreasonable phenomenon of men and women receiving different pay for the same work. In this way, we will be able in our daily economic life to undertake struggle against the notion of "males are exalted, females are demeaned."

Next, we must promote the practice of men marrying and moving into women's households where there are only daughters but no sons. So doing can serve, in actual practice, to dispel the anxiety of households which have only daughters but no sons and to struggle against the notion that "of the three unfilial acts, the worst is to have no son." In addition, other measures which cannot be listed here one by one should also be adopted.

In their adoption, these various measures must be, on the one hand, widely discussed by the masses and argued "out through airing views in a big way or maybe in a small way" so that they can penetrate deeply into people's hearts and turn into voluntary acts of the masses. On the other hand, the state and the collectives must follow Chairman Mao's instruction: "Changing old customs should also be included in the plans to be drawn up" (Mao, 1977: 487-88), and include these measures in their plans, grasping them firmly and well.

We firmly believe that Marxism is invincible, that the ideology of the proletariat will indeed defeat the way of Confucius and Mencius, that the new socialist style will indeed triumph over old traditions and old habits, and that family planning will indeed supplant the anarchic state of childbearing.

II. The guiding principle for the practice of family planning

Our nation's guiding principle for the practice of family planning is the principle of unity between state guidance and mass voluntarism. The reason that we are able to put this principle into effect is that in our country the interests of the masses of people and the interests of the state are fundamentally the same. The state's promotion of family planning proceeds from the interests of the masses, and for that reason, family planning is able to have the support of the masses and to become the voluntary act of the masses. The principle of unity between state guidance and mass voluntarism not only embodies the fundamental interests of a proletarian state, but also expresses the need and desire of the masses of the people.

The principle of unity between state guidance and mass voluntarism is a unified principle which demands guidance from the Party and the state as well as an increase in voluntarism on the part of the masses. The absence of either component will not do. This is precisely the same as Chairman Mao's earnest advice: "We must have faith in the masses and we must have faith in the Party. These are two cardinal principles. If we doubt these principles, we shall accomplish nothing" (Mao, 1977: 188). With state guidance, but without the voluntary participation of the masses, family planning has no mass foundation and cannot succeed. Conversely, even though voluntarism among the masses is very high, family planning will be difficult to realize if the necessary state guidance and clearly outlined directions and goals do not exist.

To firmly uphold State guidance is mainly:

(i) To carry through earnestly the various important instructions of Chairman Mao, Premier Zhou, and Chairman Hua concerning late marriage and family planning and the general and specific policies on late marriage and family planning formulated by the Party's Central Committee under the leadership of Chairman Hua. On the matter of late marriage, Chairman Mao had already issued a series of important instructions, e.g., the instructions that

> young people between fourteen and twenty-five (should) keep fit, study well, and work well (Mao, 1977: 96-7);

that

> as far as procreation is concerned, the human race has been in a state of total anarchy and has failed to exercise control (is unacceptable) (Mao, 1977: 488);

that

> in densely populated regions, (it is necessary to) spread family planning step by step until family planning gradually becomes universal (to achieve) the complete realization of family planning in the future (Mao, 1977: 488);

that

> there should also be a ten-year program for family planning;

that in carrying out family planning,

> it is necessary to try it out in selected places and then spread it step by step;

that

> family planning requires open education, which simply means airing views freely and holding great debates;

that the realization of family planning must follow the mass line: it

> will be out of the question without the weight of society as a whole behind it . . . or without general consent and joint effort;

and that family planning

> should not be promoted in the minority nationality areas or in sparsely populated regions. (Mao, 1977: 488)

In these instructions of Chairman Mao, the Party and state guidelines for family planning work are fully embodied. Chairman Hua instructed, "we surely must always hold high and resolutely defend the flag of Chairman Mao" (Hua, 1977: 2). Therefore, insistence on state guidance means that we must first hold high the flag of Chairman Mao and resolutely carry through and realize Chairman Mao's instructions on family planning work.

(ii) The spread of family planning work must employ the national population plan as its foundation and goal. In the national population plan are embodied the knowledge and application, on the part of the state, of the law of socialist human reproduction and the national policy for planned population growth. Therefore, as far as family planning work is concerned, the population plan embodies a concentrated reflection of state guidance and should be the basis for family planning work and the aim of the struggle. Any family planning work that deviates from the population plan will inevitably lose its direction and goal.

(iii) State guidance also embodies concrete details for family planning work from the scientific and technical standpoints. It includes support for and guarantee of expenses, medical personnel, and material supplies on the part of the state.

Insistence on mass voluntarism means that we must fully believe in the masses, rely on the masses, and mobilize the masses. It means that we hand the goals of the family planning policy and the population plan over to the masses, teach them to understand correctly the meaning of family planning, and arouse in them initiative and voluntarism. As long as the masses possess the correct appreciation and grasp the policy, they will develop a great deal of socialist initiative and voluntarily respond to the call of the state for late marriage and family planning. They will choose family planning measures according to personal circumstances, turning family planning into a voluntary and conscious act.

We must have a full and correct understanding of the principle of unity between state guidance and mass voluntarism. State guidance absolutely does not depend simply on administrative fiats, which we consistently oppose. Mass voluntarism certainly is not a *laissez-faire* policy or a policy of let things drift where they may. In essence, the implementation of the principle of unity between state guidance and mass voluntarism in family planning work is both to strengthen the Party's leadership, insisting upon politics in command, and to mobilize the masses, organizing an extensive mass movement. To strengthen the Party's leadership, the key lies in the effective implementation of the Party's general and specific policies on family planning. To insist on politics in command is to oppose the view that family planning is an unimportant family chore or a purely technical task, and to grasp family planning as a major task connected to socialist construction as well as a major task in the superstructure of socialist revolution. To organize an extensive mass movement is to insist on the mass line in family planning work. Family planning is a major task for hundreds of millions of people. Without undertaking a mass movement, without explaining its rationale clearly to the masses, and without bringing into full play the initiative and creativity of the masses, family planning will not develop well.

On the basis of insistence on the principle of unity between state guidance and mass voluntarism, various localities in our country have gained a great deal of good experience in grasping family planning work well. Such experiences can be summed up as follows:

(a) The key to grasping family planning work well lies in the fact that Party committees at all levels attach importance to it and make it the order of the day. Chairman Mao and Premier Zhou both deemed family planning important and issued a series of instructions about it. Chairman Hua also views family planning as an important matter and has issued instructions many times. Party leadership at all levels must also attach importance to this work and tackle it. "By 'tackling it' I mean that it must be put on the agenda and studied." (Mao, 1977: 435)

But, it is not enough only to attach importance to it and tackle it. We must tackle it diligently. Chairman Mao said, "Whatever the matter may be, only if we tackle it diligently and do not let up can we have a firm hold on it" (Mao, 1960: 1332). Family planning work is no exception. Party committees at all levels "cannot but tackle it and do so without letup" (*Ibid.*). Of course, while Party committees at all levels should tackle family planning work diligently, this does not mean holding discussions or drafting resolutions daily. Party committees have a thousand things to attend to; the tasks must have different priorities and varying weight and urgency. The so-called "tackling it without letup" means none other than several serious discussions each year as well as several evaluations each year.

Stressing that there is too much work and that there is no time to take up everything is incorrect. Revolution always entails a busy schedule; carrying out socialism in a big way means an even busier schedule. The important point is, as per Chairman Mao's instruction, that we must master the "piano playing" work method. That is to say, "Party committees must grasp the core tasks as well as simultaneously undertake other tasks around the core tasks" (Mao, 1960: 1332). Therefore, the kind of belief that places core tasks and family planning work in opposition to one another is also incorrect. Today, in our nation's vast countryside, the core task is "in agriculture, learn from Tazhai" and the spread of the Tazhai experience. But, "in agriculture, learn from Tazhai" work and family planning work in no way contradict each other. Doing good work in family planning is both to release the labor power of women and to guarantee the march of all women commune members capable of labor to the front line of agriculture. All this will greatly accelerate the deep thrust of the movement of "in agriculture, learn from Tazhai," In so doing, agriculture production will develop according to plan. It will then be possible to set aside a still larger volume of grain to be sold to the state, to add still more to collective accumulation, and to raise more quickly the peasants' standard of living. Contributions to the state and to the collectives will thus be greatly enhanced. Therefore, in the course of tackling the core tasks of "in agriculture, learn from Tazhai," Party committees at all levels in the villages should spare no effort simultaneously to achieve good results in family planning work.

(b) Extensive, far-reaching, and persistent family planning propaganda and education work should be developed: (1) to disseminate the instructions on family planning issued by Chairman Mao,

Premier Zhou, and the Party's Central Committee under the leadership of Chairman Hua so that the great masses can receive an education in Chairman Mao's revolutionary line; (2) to disseminate the proletarian viewpoint on marriage and childbearing and to criticize the way of Confucius and Mencius so that the great masses can receive an education in the proletarian viewpoint regarding marriage and childbearing; (3) to employ films, radio broadcasts, slides, exhibits, and pamphlets to disseminate knowledge of physiology and scientific contraceptive methods widely so that the great masses can receive an education in the laws of human reproductive physiology; (4) to undertake, in accordance with Chairman Mao's instructions, the task of disseminating to middle school students information on physiology and hygiene during puberty and educating them on late marriage. "To conduct patient, lively, and easily understood propaganda and education" among the masses in these subjects, we must rely on propaganda's "great power of persuasion" and prevent "trying to subdue their audience by threatening to stick labels on them." (Mao, 1977: 262)

(c) Mobilize fully and rely on the masses in doing good family planning work. Family planning is a matter of concern to the masses. A great deal of work must rely on the masses and the advanced elements among them. In production brigades and production teams, the extensive installation of "elder sisters-in-law" as brigade or team leaders is a good practice. Assign them family planning policy decisions, instructions, and work; and let them form close contact with the masses of women. Given their familiarity with the circumstances of their localities, family planning can be developed smoothly. In family planning, reliance on the masses requires the grooming of a great many activists among young women as well as among male comrades, because the implementation of family planning is a joint effort of both men and women. Party and Youth League members must bring into full play their leadership role. Party Committees at all levels should enlist the masses in fostering persons who serve as advanced models in family planning, and let the models carry the message. When the examples are displayed, everybody will know the direction.

(d) The close cooperation and the common effort of all departments and all quarters are the key conditions for achieving good results in family planning work. Family planning is a matter of concern to the whole nation, and hence is also the common duty of all departments and units. Industrial enterprises, commercial enterprises, scientific, educational, cultural, and health units as well as labor unions, associations of poor people, the Youth League, and propaganda units at all levels should view family planning as their common duty and should all make the necessary contributions to the cause of positively advancing family planning work. Industrial departments should positively produce contraceptives, guarantee their supply, and satisfy the needs of medical departments. Commercial departments should take the initiative in keeping in touch with industrial departments, positively organizing the flow of goods and materials, and undertake the distribution of contraceptives free of charge and their delivery to households. Scientific departments should strive to ascend scientific peaks, marching forward in work production, research, and test production of more effective and more convenient contraceptive compounds which have fewer side effects. Educational departments must thoroughly educate students, stressing the transformation of the youths' world outlook. At the same time, they must actively edit middle-school textbooks on physiology and hygiene to enable students to understand, while still in school, human reproductive physiology and the meaning of late marriage and family planning. Cultural departments must strengthen their use of various artistic forms to propagandize late marriage and family planning in order to create among the masses of the people an image depicting the glory of late marriage and family planning and to allow the notion of late marriage and family planning to penetrate deeply into the minds of the people. The burden on the shoulders of the health departments is even heavier: they must actively provide guidance on scientific contraceptive methods, help the vast number of villages to train large numbers of "barefoot doctors" and family planning medical personnel, and do research on scientific contraceptive methods. All mass organizations should conscientiously shoulder the tasks of late marriage and family planning propaganda and strive to do it well. As all departments ever more ably fulfill their own responsibilities, our nation's family planning work will register still greater gains.

III. With class struggle as the framework, firmly adhere to the Party's basic line and achieve family planning

During the historical stage of socialism, the sphere of marriage and childbearing, just as in other spheres, is full of acute class struggle. The adoption of family planning is a profound socialist revolution in the ideological sphere, as well as a broad struggle between two classes, two roads, and two lines in the sphere of marriage and childbearing. Therefore, to achieve good results in family planning work, we must use class struggle as the framework and firmly adhere to the Party's basic line in carrying on our determined struggle against class enemies in society and against bourgeois representatives in the Party.

The defeated class enemies will certainly not take their defeat willingly. They will always employ all means and search out every opportunity to create chaos and destruction, vainly trying to upset our nation's socialist system under the dictatorship of the proletariat. In the sphere of family planning, some class enemies spread the decadent way of life of the bourgeois class, ingratiate themselves with and corrupt youths, deceive youths into falling in love and marrying early, and compete with the proletariat for successors. Some class enemies carry on marriage sales in a disguised form, disrupt late marriage, and swindle money from people. Some class enemies spread rumors to confuse people, vilify scientific contraceptive methods, and disrupt family planning. Some class enemies carry on feudal superstitious activities, incite the masses into praying to gods and drawing divination sticks in temples, and encourage blind reproduction. Of the disruptive activities of the class enemies against late marriage and family planning, the most common are those that prey on the old thoughts and old concepts which remain in the minds of the people; and they use the old customs and old habits in their continued proclamation of the way of Confucius and Mencius. They either nakedly or in camouflage spread "fatalism," publicize "males are exalted, females are demeaned," boost "the more the sons, the more blessings," and continue to poison the masses of people.

To counteract the criminal activities of the class enemies in society against late marriage and family planning, we must mercilessly expose and resolutely attack them, mobilize the masses, and practice the dictatorship of the proletariat to guarantee the smooth advancement of family planning work. This is because, during the entire historical period of socialism, "the class struggle between the proletariat and the bourgeoisie, the class struggle between the various political forces, and the class struggle between the proletariat and the bourgeoisie in the ideological field will still be protracted and tortuous and at times even very sharp" (Mao, 1977: 409). We must be well prepared for a long struggle, constantly be on guard, and always be prepared. Whenever class enemies disrupt and do damage, we will be able to strike back at them in time. The kind of belief that treats family planning work as merely technical work of an administrative nature clearly is divorced from the over-all framework of class struggle. For this reason, it is harmful and erroneous.

Chairman Hua has pointed out, "Class struggle in society is still being waged daily and hourly. The struggle between the two lines within the Party still reflects the class struggle in society at large and is an undiluted reflection thereof" (Hua, 1977: 17). The anti-late marriage and anti-family planning class struggle in society at large is necessarily reflected and concentrated in the two-line struggle within the Party. The representatives of the bourgeois class inside the Party, Liu Shaoqi, Lin Biao, and Wang, Zhang, Jiang, and Yao pushed the counterrevolutionary revisionist line, vainly tried to usurp the supreme powers of the Party and the state and to substitute the dictatorship of the bourgeoisie for the dicta-torship of the proletariat. They took advantage of illegally obtained powers to issue instructions and to pen comments on documents, mixing right and wrong, creating confusion, and interfering in and damaging late marriage and family planning work. All this is part of their counterrevolutionary criminal activities.

This bunch of representatives of the bourgeoisies inside the Party were opposed to Chairman Mao's instructions that youths should postpone marriage, and they incited young men and women to marry early, spreading the nonsense that "early marriage is good; by marrying early and having children early, you will not be old when your children grow up." They vainly tried to restrict our nation's vast number of youths to the narrow confines of the fam-ily in order to realize their scheme.

Liu Shaoqi openly opposed Chairman Mao's instruction that to implement family planning will require open education and de-creed, "do not undertake a campaign to mobilize and propagan-dize family planning in the villages," "do not make reports on fam-ily planning at mass meetings." He vainly tried to isolate and cold-shoulder family planning so as to let it disappear of its own accord.

Liu Shaoqi and Lin Biao were both opposed to Chairman Mao's instruction on bringing into full play the role of women in carrying "one-half of the sky," and strenuously attempted to peddle the feudal ethic of "males are exalted, females are demeaned." They uttered such nonsense as "the husband's destiny determines the wife's destiny," "women's energy should be devoted to their husbands," and women should "hold the shopping basket, stay by the stove, carry the children, wait on old men, and become model wives." Under our nation's socialist system, the destiny of the vast number of women certainly is not determined by the destiny of their husbands, but tied to the destiny of the dictatorship of the proletariat. Women's energy should be devoted, first of all, to revolution and productive labor. What they should consider before all else is: make more contributions to the state and the collective. Today, vast numbers of urban and rural women are members of the ranks of people energetically working and producing in order to become Tazhai or Daqing types of people. The erroneous notion of "males are exalted, females are demeaned" disseminated by Liu Shaoqi and Lin Biao is diametrically opposed to the complete emancipation of women and a vain attempt to have women, who constitute one-half of the population, return to the kitchen and once again sink down to the level of the family's slave and servant and a machine for bearing and rearing children, totally divorced from the Three Great Revolutionary Practices.

Jiang Qing, acting against the respected Premier Zhou with her typical aggressive design of a wolverine, was strenuously opposed to the practice, long advocated by Premier Zhou, of propagandizing family planning through the use of films and other art forms. She once wrote on a report the comment, "Use of films to propagandize family planning is inappropriate." Films publicizing family planning were thereupon prohibited from being shown to the masses. This seriously interfered with and damaged propaganda and education work in family planning. Jiang Qing, in order to usurp the powers of the Party's leadership and ascend to the throne of "dowager," also assumed the style of a theorist and uttered the nonsense "women are production forces," "in the production forces, women are the most basic," "men are also borne by women," etc., casually treating women's reproductive power and social production forces as one and the same thing. According to Jiang Qing's logic, so long as women bear many children, they will expand the social production forces. In this way women would never be able to cast off their unreasonable role "of family slave-servant and breeding machine," and the control of population growth would become the control of the increase in social production forces. This is certainly ridiculous to the extreme. This self-appointed representative of women, Jiang Qing, actually is the most vicious enemy of the masses of women.

The "gang of four" severely damaged late marriage and family planning. They confused people's thinking, disrupted the revolutionary order, fostered the forces of capitalism, and helped to incite the clamor of the class enemies. In areas and units in which they had extended their hands, the phenomena of early marriage and blind reproduction reached serious proportions.

Chairman Hua has instructed,

> At present, the whole Party, the whole army, and all of the nation's nationalities should continue to extend deeply the great political revolution of exposing and criticizing the "gang of four," further strengthen the dictatorship of the proletariat, and fully and correctly carry out Chairman Mao's revolutionary line in the political, economic, and cultural spheres in order to attain order and peace everywhere." (Hua, 1977: 28)

In the sphere of family planning, in order to carry through Chairman Mao's revolutionary line comprehensively and correctly, we must expose and criticize intensively the criminal acts of the "gang of four" against late marriage and family planning. Only when the criminal acts of the "gang of four" are exposed and criticized thoroughly and their interferences and obstructions cleared, can we guarantee that family planning will proceed in the direction pointed out by Chairman Mao's revolutionary line, attain universal planned births, and realize planned population growth.

REFERENCES

*(*Item published in Chinese)*

Atlas Publishing Co. (1972) *World Atlas*, Peking.

*Lenin, I. (1959) *Complete Works of Lenin*, Peking: People's Publishing Co., Vol. XIX.

* _____ (1972) *Selected Works of Lenin*, Peking: People's Publishing Co., Vol. V.

*Hua Guofeng (1977) *To Carry on to the End the Continuing Revolution under the Dictatorship of the Proletariat*, Peking: People's Publishing Co.

* _____ (1977) "Mobilize the Whole Party to Greatly Promote Agriculture," *Red Flag* 1(January): 42-55.

*Marx, Karl, and Frederick Engels (1956, 1960, 1972, 1971) *The Complete Works of Marx and Engels*, Peking: People's Publishing Co., Vols. I, III, XXIV, and XXXV.

* _____ (1972) *Selected Works of Marx and Engels*, Peking: People's Publishing Co., Vol. IV.

*Mao, Zedong (1956) *High Tide of Socialism in China's Villages*, Peking: People's Publishing Co., Vol. II.

* _____ (1964) *Selected Readings from the Works of Mao Tse-tung*, Peking: People's Publishing Co., Vol. I.

* _____ (1969) *Selected Works of Mao Tse-tung*, Peking: People's Publishing Co., Vol. IV.

* _____ (1977) *Selected Works of Mao Tse-tung*, Peking: Foreign Languages Press, Vol. V.

Mussolini, B. (1927) "Number Is Power," n.s.

New Time (1974) No. 23:33.

People's China (1972) No. 1:85.

People's Daily (Renmin ribao) April 17, 1973
                                October 1, 1973
                                July 6, 1977
                                July 15, 1977.

Shirer, William (1960) *The Rise and Fall of the Third Reich*, New York: Simon-Shuster.

Vogt, William (1948) *The Road of Survival*, New York: W. Sloane Associates.

*Wu, Xiyung (1936) *The History of Population Thought*, Peiping: University of Peiping Press.

Appendices

A. Mao Zedong on Accumulation and Consumption*

. . . When the people overthrew the rule of imperialism, feudalism and bureaucrat-capitalism, many were not clear as to which way China should head—toward capitalism or toward socialism. Facts have now provided the answer: Only socialism can save China. The socialist system has promoted the rapid development of the productive forces of our country, a fact even our enemies abroad have had to acknowledge.

But our socialist system has only just been set up; it is not yet fully established or fully consolidated. In joint state-private industrial and commercial enterprise, capitalists still get a fixed rate of interest on their capital, that is to say, exploitation still exists. So far as ownership is concerned, these enterprises are not yet completely socialist in nature. A number of our agricultural and handicraft producers' cooperatives are still semi-socialist, while even in the fully socialist cooperatives certain specific problems of ownership remain to be solved. Relations between production and exchange in accordance with socialist principles are being gradually established within and between all branches of our economy, and more and more appropriate forms are being sought. The problem of the proper relation of accumulation to consumption within each of the two sectors of the socialist economy—the one where the means of production are owned by the whole people and the other where the means of production are owned by the collective —and the problem of the proper relation of accumulation to consumption between the two sectors themselves are complicated problems for which it is not easy to work out a perfectly rational

*From Mao's essay "On the Correct Handling of Contradictions among the People." *Selected Works of Mao Tsetung*, Vol. V, pp. 394-395. (This speech had originally been published on February 27, 1957.)

solution all at once. To sum up, socialist relations of production have been established and are in correspondence with the growth of the productive forces, but these relations are still far from perfect, and this imperfection stands in contradiction to the growth of the productive forces. Apart from correspondence as well as contradiction between the relations of production and the growth of the productive forces, there is correspondence as well as contradiction between the superstructure and the economic base. The superstructure, comprising the state system and laws of the people's democratic dictatorship and the socialist ideology guided by Marxism-Leninism, plays a positive role in facilitating the victory of socialist transformation and the socialist way of organizing labor; it is in correspondence with the socialist economic base, that is, with socialist relations of production. But the existence of bourgeois ideology, a certain bureaucratic style of work in our state organs and defects in some of the links in our state institutions are in contradiction with the socialist economic base. We must continue to resolve all such contradictions in the light of our specific conditions. Of course, new problems will emerge as these contradictions are resolved. And further efforts will be required to resolve the new contradictions. For instance, a constant process of readjustment through state planning is needed to deal with the contradiction between production and the needs of society, which will long remain an objective reality. Every year our country draws up an economic plan in order to establish a proper ratio between accumulation and consumption and achieve an equilibrium between production and needs. Equilibrium is nothing but a temporary, relative, unity of opposites. By the end of each year, this equilibrium, taken as a whole, is upset by the struggle of opposites; the unity undergoes a change, equilibrium becomes disequilibrium, unity becomes disunity, and once again it is necessary to work out an equilibrium and unity for the next year. Herein lies the superiority of our planned economy. As a matter of fact, this equilibrium, this unity, is partially upset every month or every quarter, and partial readjustments are called for. Sometimes, contradictions arise and the equilibrium is upset because our subjective arrangements do not conform to objective reality; this is what we call making a mistake. The ceaseless emergence and ceaseless resolution of contradictions constitute the dialectical law of the development of things. . . .

B. Mao Zedong on the Necessity of Birth Control*

... In my opinion, China must depend on intensive cultivation to feed itself. One day China will become the world's number one high-yield country. Some of our counties are already producing one thousand catties per *mou*. Will it be possible to reach two thousand catties per *mou* in half a century? In future will it be possible for the region north of the Yellow River to produce eight hundred catties per *mou*, that north of the Huai River one thousand catties and that south of it two thousand? There are still a few decades left before these targets are reached at the beginning of the twenty-first century, or maybe it won't take that long. We depend on intensive cultivation to feed ourselves, and even with a fairly large population we still have enough food. I think an average of three *mou* of land per person is more than enough and in future less than one *mou* will yield enough grain to feed one individual. Of course birth control will still be necessary, and I am not encouraging more births.

Please investigate how much grain the peasants actually consume. We must encourage diligence and thrift in running the household and economy in the use of grain so as to have reserves. When the state has a reserve and each cooperative and family has one too, we shall be quite well off with these three kinds of reserves. Otherwise, if all the grain is eaten up, what prosperity will there be to speak of?

*From Mao's essay "Be Activists in Promoting the Revolution." *Selected Works of Mao Tsetung*, Vol. V, pp. 486-488 (a speech delivered on October 9, 1957, at the Enlarged Third Plenary Session of the Eight Central Committee of the Chinese Communist Party). [This is the first appearance in Mao's writings of a specific reference to birth control—H.Y.T.]

This year there should be a little more accumulation wherever a good harvest has been reaped or natural disasters have not occurred. It is most necessary to make up for possible shortages with surpluses. In cooperatives in some provinces, in addition to the accumulation fund (5 percent), the public welfare fund (5 percent) and management expenses, production costs account for 20 percent of the total value of output, and capital construction expenditures in turn account for 20 percent of production costs. I discussed the matter with comrades from other provinces, who said these capital construction expenditures were probably a bit too high. What I am saying today is to be taken as suggestions, which you may carry out if feasible, otherwise not. Moreover, it is not necessary for all provinces and counties to act in exactly the same way, and I leave the matter to you for consideration. The management expenses of cooperatives in some places have so far assumed too large a proportion and should therefore be reduced to 1 percent. They consist of allowances to cadres of cooperatives plus administrative expenses. They should be cut and capital expenditures on farmlands increased. . . .

There should also be a ten-year program for family planning. However, it should not be promoted in the minority nationality areas or in sparsely populated regions. Even in densely populated regions it is necessary to try it out in selected places and then spread it step by step until family planning gradually becomes universal. Family planning requires open education, which simply means airing views freely and holding great debates. As far as procreation is concerned, the human race has been in a state of total anarchy and has failed to exercise control. The complete realization of family planning in the future will be out of the question without the weight of society as a whole behind it, that is, without general consent and joint effort. . . .

C. Mao Zedong on the Health of Young People *

Young people between fourteen and twenty-five need to study and work, but as youth is the age of physical growth, much is imperiled if their health is neglected. The young need to study much more, for they have to learn many things older people already know. However, they must not be overloaded with either study or work. And the fourteen-to eighteen-year-olds in particular should not be made to work with the same intensity as grown-ups. Young people, being what they are, need more time for play, recreation and sports. Otherwise they won't be happy. And in time they will fall in love and get married. In all this they are different from older people.

I would like to say a few words to our young people: first, I wish them good health; second, I wish them success in their study; and third, I wish them success in their work. . . .

In short, young people should be enabled to keep fit, study well and work well. Some leading comrades are interested only in getting work out of young people and pay little attention to their health. You can quote the above to their faces. You are on firm ground, namely, you are protecting the younger generation so that it can grow sturdily. We of the older generation were deprived of our due, for adults simply didn't bother themselves about their children. Adults had a table to eat their meals at while children had to do without one. Children had no say in the family, and if they cried they were sure to get slapped. In the new China of today we must change our approach and think more in the interest of our children and youth.

*From Mao's speech on "The Youth League in Its Work Must Take the Characteristics of Youth into Consideration." *Selected Works of Mao Tse-tung*, Vol. V, pp. 96-97 (a talk on June 30, 1953, when Mao received the Presidium of the Second National Congress of the Democratic Youth League of China). [Even though these words provide the basic rationale for China's late marriage policy, Mao did not, on this or any other occasion, specifically mention the link between health and the desirability of late marriage—H.Y.T.]

D. *Chi Lung* / China Explains Her Views on the Population Question*

Chi Lung, Deputy Representative of the Chinese Delegation to the 29th Session of the United Nations Economic Commission for Asia and the Far East (ECAFE), made a speech on the population question at the April 16 meeting of the Committee of the Whole.

Basic cause of poverty and backwardness

"The Delegation of the People's Republic of China," he said, "would like to explain here our views on the population question and to hold consultations together with the delegations of other countries."

Chi Lung went on: "We hold that, of all things in the world, people are the most precious. People are the decisive factor in the social productive forces. They are first of all producers and then consumers. As producers, they ceaselessly concentrate on production in breadth and depth and can produce more products than they consume. Under certain socio-historical conditions, some problems may arise as the population increases. This is caused by various obstacles blocking the development of the social productive forces. The entire progress of history shows that people are always able to sweep aside obstacles in the way of advance, promote the steady development of the social productive forces and create more and more wealth for society. Those views which regard people as a negative factor, that people are purely consumers and that growth in population means an obstacle to economic development do not correspond to the historical facts in the development of mankind. Those views which claim that efforts to reduce the

Peking Review, No. 17 (April 27, 1973).

population's mortality rate would harm the socio-economic progress are even more absurd.

"We hold that the fundamental reason for the present poverty and backwardness in many developing countries in the Asian and Far East region as well as in other regions lies in the policies of aggression, plunder and war pushed by imperialism, colonialism and neo-colonialism and in particular by the superpowers which seriously destroy these countries' productive forces. The decisive conditions for changing this situation of poverty and backwardness are to get rid of aggression and oppression by imperialism, colonialism and neo-colonialism, to combat big-power hegemonism and power politics, to strive for and safeguard national independence and to develop the national economy independently. In our view, it is erroneous to say that the poverty and backwardness of the developing countries stem mainly from over-population and that a population policy is of fundamental significance and plays the main role in solving the problem of poverty and backwardness."

Malthusians refuted

Referring to the Chinese people's own experience, Chi Lung said: "Old China's poverty and backwardness is known to all. Under the leadership of the Communist Party of China headed by Chairman Mao Tsetung, the Chinese people, after a long and valiant struggle, overthrew the reactionary rule of imperialism and its lackeys, founded the People's Republic of China and are engaged in socialist economic construction independently, self-reliantly and in a planned way. Though our population has increased relatively quickly since the founding of the People's Republic of China, the increase in production was even faster. Over the past 24 years, China's population grew from more than 500 million to over 700 million, an increase of more than 50 percent, but during the same period, grain production more than doubled, increasing from 110 million tons to 240 million tons; cloth and other light industrial products increased by several fold, some even by more than ten-fold; and still bigger increases have been registered in heavy industrial products. A look at the average annual rate of progressive increase since the founding of the People's Republic of China shows that the average annual progressive increase in population is about 2 percent while that of grain is nearly 4 percent, with the average annual progressive increase for the last decade being about 5 percent. Moreover, at present China's cultivated land (which is roughly over 100 million hectares) only amounts to a little more than 15 percent of the total area of the country. The per-hectare yield for grain is still not high and mechanization in grain production is still at a very low level. Ranging from whatever angle, there are enormous potentialities for China's grain production which will grow too slowly. China is a developing country and the living standards of her people are still rather low. However, starvation and unemployment have been eliminated. There is food, clothing and work for the people. Some Malthusians have prated that when there are too many people, the question of feeding them cannot be solved, that too many people obstruct the progress of society, and so on. Facts have thoroughly refuted such nonsense."

China's population policy

"Population increase in a planned way is China's published policy. We follow such a policy not because the question of 'over-population' exists in China. In China, social production is carried out in a planned way and this requires that the population increase is planned, too. It is also necessary to have a planned population increase in order to promote the thorough emancipation of women, care for mothers and women and children and bring up and educate the younger generation well, and improve the people's health and bring about national prosperity. Such a policy conforms with the interests and aspirations of the broad masses.

"To implement the policy of planned population increase requires us to develop medical and health work throughout the cities and countryside and do a good job in maternity and child care on the basis of actively developing production and raising the people's living standards and, while lowering the mortality rate of the population on the one hand, practice planned childbirth on the other to regulate the birthrate. What we mean by planned childbirth is not only birth control, but adopting different measures according to different circumstances. In densely populated areas with high birthrates, we advocate late marriage and birth control, so that the age difference between the parents and their children will be about 30 years rather than about 20 years. In national minority areas and other sparsely populated areas, we adopt appropriate measures to help increase population and promote production; guidance and help are also given to those who desire to practice birth control.

"China's work on birth control is carried out under the principle of voluntariness on the part of the masses with state guidance. The government and social organizations at all levels mobilize the masses to practice planned childbirth voluntarily through widespread propaganda and education. The state provides contraceptives free of charge and related medical services. To the few cases of sterility, active treatment is also given.

"China has gained rather noteworthy success in lowering the population's mortality rate. Initial success has also been obtained in birth-control work in the densely populated areas, but it is not developing evenly. A change has been brought about in the national minority areas where the population of some nationalities had in the past shown a sharp decline due to brutal persecution by the reactionary forces. The population in these areas has shown a fairly rapid increase and now there is a growing population and developing production. Our experience in planned childbirth is still not sufficient and we must continue in our efforts. Facts prove that our country is able to gradually achieve the control of population growth by mankind itself in a planned way."

Chi Lung added: "We hold that the drawing up of a population policy is the internal affair of the various countries. Conditions differ in the various countries, so we cannot seek a forcibly uniform policy on population. Under the premise of full respect for the sovereignty of the various countries and in accordannce with the wishes of their people, it is of course beneficial to exchange experience internationally on the problems of population and family planning. We are ready to learn from the fine experience of the people of other countries."

E. *Yu Wang* / Chinese Observer on the Population Question*

The question of population is a question of common concern to all countries, and our country is no exception.

In old China, as a result of foreign armed aggression and long years of wars between warlords at home, diseases and epidemics were prevalent and the sick could hardly get any treatment. In those days both the birthrate and mortality rate were high, with the result that there was a low natural growth rate of population. The people were increasingly impoverished. Many workers were unemployed, the peasants went bankrupt and intellectuals could not find jobs. The broad masses of the people were living in hunger and cold. All this was caused by the ruthless oppression and plunder of imperialism, feudalism and bureaucrat-capitalism which ruined the country's social productive forces.

After the Chinese people won victory in their revolution under the leadership of Chairman Mao Tsetung and the Chinese Communist Party, they freed China from such oppression and plunder, carried out socialist construction in a planned way and put an end to famine, unemployment and other evils left over from old China.

Of all things in the world, people are the most precious. Once the people become masters of their own destiny, every miracle can be performed. As working people, human beings are first of all producers and then consumers. Having become masters of the country, the Chinese people have given play to their great initiative and creativeness, made continuous progress in production in both breadth and depth and created more and more wealth for the society.

Peking Review, No. 49 (December 7, 1973). This is a slightly abridged speech by the Chinese observer Yu Wang at the 17th session of the UN Population Commission on November 2.

Since the founding of the People's Republic of China, the rate of growth of China's production has exceeded that of her population. Over the period when the population grew by more than 50 percent from more than 500 million to over 700 million, annual grain output more than doubled, rising from 110 million tons to 250 million tons, and textile and other industrial products increased by several to over a dozen times. Take the average annual rates of growth. China's population has since the founding of New China increased around 2 percent each year while grain has on the average increased nearly 4 percent. And there are still great potentialities for an increase in China's agricultural production. At present China, a developing country, is still economically poor. The living standards of our people are still rather low. However, people are ensured of food and clothing and employment. China's vast manpower resources are being used in a planned and rational way and constitute the primary factor in the development of production. The livelihood of the Chinese people as a whole is steadily improving on the basis of the development of production.

We have learned from our own experience that it is wrong and far from the truth to say that over-population is the main cause of the poverty and backwardness of the developing countries in Asia, Africa, Latin America and that a population policy is decisive in solving the problem of poverty and backwardness.

It is evident to all that though New China has much more people than old China, the country is not poorer but richer and the people's life is improving instead of worsening. Does this not thoroughly refute those erroneous views?

Obviously, a nation cannot lift itself from poverty and backwardness and become strong and prosperous unless it breaks the shackles imposed on it by imperialism, colonialism and neo-colonialism, particularly those imposed by the superpowers, and by domestic feudalism and comprador-capitalism, attains national independence, carries out a thoroughgoing land return and develops its national economy independently.

China pursues a policy of developing its national economy in a planned way, including the policy of planned population growth. We do not approve of anarchy either in material production or in human reproduction.

Man should control himself as well as nature. In order to realize planned population growth, what we are doing is, on the basis of energetically developing production and improving the people's living standards, to develop medical and health services throughout the rural and urban areas and strengthen our work in maternity and child-care, so as to reduce the mortality rate on the one hand and regulate the birthrate by birth planning on the other.

What we mean by birth planning is not just practicing birth control, but taking different measures in the light of different circumstances. In densely populated areas where the birthrate is high, marriage at later age and birth control are advocated. However, active medical treatment is provided for those suffering from sterility. In the national minority areas and other sparsely populated areas, appropriate measures were taken to facilitate population growth and promote production. However, proper guidance and assistance were also made available to those who have too many children and desire birth control. All those who voluntarily ask for birth control are provided by the state with contraceptive drugs and relevant medical service free of charge.

Our policy benefits the building up of the country, the thorough liberation of women, the protection of mothers, women and children, the bringing up of the younger generation, and the improvement of the people's health and national prosperity. This policy is in the interests of the broad masses of the people.

In carrying out the policy of birth planning, we combine state guidance with the initiative on the part of the masses themselves. As a result of publicity and education by governments and social organization at all levels, more and more people have come to realize the importance of birth planning, and they are now practicing it of their own free will. Since birth planning is a matter of immediate concern to the broad masses, it is essential to rely on them in order to ensure success. At present we have achieved some preliminary success in this field, but progress has not been even and we have to continue our efforts.

We hold that the drawing up of a population policy is the internal affair of a country. Since conditions vary in different countries, uniformity in population policy is undesirable. However, it is of benefit to share experience and exchange ideas among countries in regard to the problem of population and birth planning on the premise of full respect for the sovereignty of all countries and in accordance with the wishes of their people. Peoples of all countries, big or small, have their own merits, and we would like to learn from them.

F. *Huang Shu-tse* / China's Views on Major Issues of World Population*

The United Nations World Population Conference opened on August 19 in Bucharest with representatives from over 130 countries and regions taking part. The opening session was addressed by President Nicolae Ceausescu of the Socialist Republic of Romania. The conference elected Romanian Foreign Minister George Macovescu, head of the Romanian delegation, president of the conference and 31 other representatives as vice-presidents. Chairman for the three committees and a working group were also elected by the conference.

The Chinese delegation was led by Huang Shu-tse and his deputy Li Ting-chuan. Huang Shu-tse spoke at the plenary meeting on August 21. Following are excerpts from his speech:

It is a pleasure for the Delegation of the People's Republic of China to be here to attend the World Population Conference and have discussions and exchange views with representatives of other countries on questions of world population.

We are sincerely glad that representatives of national-liberation movements and organizations have been invited to attend this conference as observers and we express our warm welcome to them.

The World Population Conference is being held at a time when the international situation is developing in a direction more and more favorable to the people of the world and unfavorable to imperialism, particularly the superpowers. The whole world is advancing amid great turbulence. The Sixth Special Session of the

Peking Review, No. 35 (August 30, 1974 [Excerpts]).

UN General Assembly, a session to study the problems of raw materials and development, held not long ago marked a new stage, the stage of deep-going development, in the struggle of the countries of the Third World and the people of all countries against colonialism, imperialism and hegemonism. The World Population Conference should carry on and develop the militant spirit of combating imperialism and hegemonism as manifested at the Sixth Special Session of UN General Assembly. The population problem is inseparable from political and economic problems. The Program of Action on the Establishment of an International Economic Order adopted by the UN General Assembly at its special session calls upon the World Population Conference to make its contribution to facilitating the establishment of a new international economic order. It is our hope that we representatives from different countries will make joint efforts to realize this aim. The Chinese delegation is ready to do its part toward this end. . . .

Now, the Chinese delegation would like to set forth its views and opinions on some current major issues regarding the world population.

1. Fundamental assessment of the present world population situation

Over the last few decades, along with the development of the political and economic situation in the world, there has been a fairly rapid population growth in the world, particularly in the Third World. The Third World now has a population of nearly 3,000 million, which is more than 70 percent of the world's population. How to see this fact in a correct light is the first thing we must be clear about. One superpower asserts outright that there is a "population explosion" in Asia, Africa and Latin America and that a "catastrophe to mankind" is imminent. The other superpower, while pretending at some conferences to be against Malthusianism, makes the propaganda blast that "rapid population growth is a millstone around the neck of the developing countries." Singing a duet, the two superpowers energetically try to describe the Third World's population growth as a great evil. If this fallacy is not refuted, there will be no correct point of departure in any discussion on the world population.

Of all things in the world, people are the most precious. Once the people take their destiny into their own hands, they will be able to perform miracles. Man, as worker and as creator and user of tools, is the decisive factor in the social productive forces. Man is in the first place a producer and only in the second place a consumer. Historically, the valiant, industrious and talented people of Asia, Africa and Latin America made outstanding contributions to human civilization. But over a considerable period of time, the colonialists and imperialists subjected the Asian, African and Latin American countries to brutal aggression and enslavement. They not only plundered enormous social wealth from Asia, Africa and Latin America, but also engaged in human traffic and evicted or slaughtered local inhabitants. Africa alone has lost as many as 100 million people in this way. The social productive forces in Asian, African and Latin American countries were seriously sapped. The population of some countries and nations declined drastically, and large tracts of land were laid waste. After prolonged and heroic struggles waged by the people in Asia, Africa and Latin America, a large number of countries in these regions have successively won political independence and achieved marked progress in developing their national economy and culture as compared with the past. Along with this development the population has grown rather quickly. This is not at all a bad thing but a very good thing. In the situation of "great disorder under heaven," in which the broad masses of the people are increasingly awakening, the large population of the Third World constitutes an important condition for strengthening the struggle against imperialism and hegemonism and accelerating social and economic development. Today, the people of the Third World have become the main force combating colonialism, imperialism and hegemonism and are becoming an increasingly mighty force in safeguarding national independence and developing the national economy.

It should be pointed out that on its road of advance the Third World is still confronted with numerous difficulties to be overcome through persistent struggles. The many countries that have won political independence, their economic life-lines are still controlled by colonialism and imperialism, and no fundamental change has been affected in the old economic structure. In particular, owing to intensified oppression and exploitation by the two superpowers, these countries have been unable to make full use of their vast manpower resources, and unemployment and poverty still exist there. But we are confident that the historical trend—

countries want independence, nations want liberation and the people want revolution—is irresistible. Whatever twists and turns and difficulties there may be along their road of advance, final victory belongs to the people of Asia, Africa and Latin America and of the world as a whole. On the basis of an unremitting fight against the aggression, interferences, subversion and plunder by imperialism and hegemonism and persistent defense of political and economic independence, there will arise an Asia, Africa and Latin America with a big population and a great wealth of products, where life will be abundant and culture will flourish.

The superpowers raise the false alarm of a "population explosion" and paint a depressing picture of the future of mankind. This reminds us of the notorious Malthus, who, more than 170 years ago, when the population of the world was less than 1,000 million, raised a hue and cry about "over-population" and the impossibility for the growth of production ever to catch up with that of the population. He drivelled that even with "the best directed efforts of human industry," China could hardly "double the produce . . . in any number of years." Today, the world population has more than quadrupled that of Malthus' time, but there has been much greater increase in the material wealth of society, thanks to the efforts of the broad masses of the people in surmounting numerous obstacles. In the twenty-odd years since her founding, the People's Republic of China has increased her products manyfold. The creative power of the people is boundless, and so is man's ability to exploit and utilize natural resources. The pessimistic views spread by the superpowers are utterly groundless and are being propagated with ulterior motives.

2. On the causes of the population problem and ways of solving it

At present, there is in many countries a population problem, which finds its concrete expression in unemployment, poverty, starvation, a high mortality rate, etc. The central task of our discussion at this conference should be to ascertain the causes of this problem and find ways of solving it.

The condition of the population of a country is determined by its social system and the political and economic conditions prevailing at home and internationally. Is it owing to overpopulation that unemployment and poverty exist in many countries of the world today? No, absolutely not. It is mainly due to aggression, plunder and exploitation by the imperialists, particularly the superpowers. The two superpowers are the biggest international exploiters and oppressors of today and the chief culprits responsible for unemployment and poverty in the world. The Declaration on the Establishment of a New International Economic Order adopted by the UN General Assembly at its sixth special session points out that the widening gap between the developing and the developed countries is due to the old international economic order which increasingly aggravates the inequalities, and that alien domination, foreign occupation, colonialism, racial discrimination, apartheid and neo-colonialism in all its forms are the greatest obstacles to the full emancipation and progress of the developing countries. In our opinion, the primary way of solving the population problem lies in combating the aggression and plunder by the imperialists, colonialists and neo-colonialists, and particularly the superpowers, breaking down the unequal international economic relations, winning and safeguarding national independence, and developing the national economy and culture independently and self-reliantly in the light of each country's specific conditions and differing circumstances and raising the living standards of the people.

It is well known that large numbers of relative surplus population and widespread poverty exist in the superpower countries too. In one superpower country millions are jobless and tens of millions live in poverty. And in the other, which flaunts the label of socialism, the gap between the rich privileged stratum and the poor working people grows wider and wider, the bureaucrat monopoly capitalists fire workers at will, and the livelihood of the broad masses of workers is insecure. This state of affairs is wholly the result of the ruthless oppression and exploitation which the superpowers practice at home.

In recent years, the struggle of the Third World against imperialism and hegemonism has been surging forward vigorously, and the struggle of the people in the developed countries and the superpower countries against ruthless oppression and exploitation is on the upsurge. These two irresistible tides converging together are even more powerfully pounding at and shaking the foundations of imperialism and hegemonism, thus paving the way for the eradication of unemployment and poverty throughout the world.

The two superpowers are most afraid that the real cause of unemployment and poverty should be uncovered and that the broad masses should clearly see the correct way of solving this problem. So they have concocted various fallacies which they loudly and repeatedly propagate everywhere.

The claim that "over-population is the reason why the have-not countries are poor" is a worn-out tune of the superpowers. What a mass of figures they have calculated in order to prove that population is too large, the food supply too small and natural resources insufficient! But they never calculate the amount of natural resources they have plundered, the social wealth they have grabbed and the super-profits they have extorted from Asia, Africa and Latin America. Should an account be made of their exploitation, the truth with regard to the population problem will at once be out. Their multitude of population statistics will not help them a bit either. The average population to a square kilometer is only 12 in Africa, and 15 in Latin America. Though population density in the developing countries of Asia is a bit higher, it is nonetheless lower than that in the developed countries of Western Europe. How can it be said then that the have-not countries are poor because of over-population? They claim that poverty can be overcome by reducing the rate of population growth. If so, why are there still so many jobless and underfed people in the two superpower countries where the rate of population growth is relatively low and population density fairly small?

Social-imperialism asserts that "only economic development with my aid can solve your population problem." This is a ruse. It goes without saying that economic development is necessary for a country to emerge from poverty and solve its population problems. The point is that what social-imperialism calls "economic development" is nothing but a fraud, as it is not coupled with the fight against imperialism and hegemonism and a change in the unequal international economic relations. Let us ask: Don't you talk glibly of "economic development"? Why do you fly into a rage at the mention of establishing a new international economic order? Why do you try your utmost to maintain the old international economic relations and obstruct the economic development of the Third World countries? Don't you talk glibly of "aid"? Why do you take advantage of others' difficulties to reap fabulous profits, relentlessly press for the repayment of loans and practice blackmail? In practicing neo-colonialism, you have outdone the other superpower. Your so-called "aid" can only mean intensified control and plunder of the Third World countries, with the consequent aggravation of their unemployment and poverty.

The allegation that "over-population in the developing countries is threatening the security of the world" is a completely false accusation that reverses right and wrong. One may ask: Was it over-population that led to the wars in Indochina, the Middle East and other areas or to the armed occupation of Czechoslovakia? Is it owing to over-population that oppressed nations and oppressed people have carried out just wars for independence and liberation? No, wars of aggression are launched by the imperialists, particularly the superpowers.

The deplorable conditions of unemployment and poverty in old China are universally known. Under the leadership of Chairman Mao Tsetung and the Chinese Communist Party, the Chinese people, through a prolonged struggle, overthrew imperialism, feudalism and bureaucrat-capitalism which weighed on them like three big mountains, and have since carried on socialist revolution and socialist construction and in relatively short time succeeded in eliminating unemployment left over from old China. In the twenty-odd years since the founding of the People's Republic, China's population has increased nearly 60 percent, from about 500 million to nearly 800 million. Yet, in the same period, annual grain output has more than doubled, rising from 110 million to 250 million tons, and the output of textiles and other industrial products has increased manyfold. At present, the area under cultivation in China is only slightly more than 10 percent of her total territory. There are enormous potentialities untapped since there remain vast areas to be reclaimed, and the per hectare yield can still be greatly raised. At present the living standards of our people are still rather low, yet everyone is ensured of employment, food and clothing, and the livelihood of the people is steadily improving. The broad masses of the Chinese people have never displayed such a high degree of initiative and creativeness. In building socialism, China's vast manpower resources are being used in a planned and rational way. Facts of China's history have completely exploded the various fallacies spread by the superpowers with regard to the population problem and fully borne out "the truth that revolution plus production can solve the problem of feeding the population," as set forth by Chairman Mao Tsetung.

3. On the formulation and implementation of a population policy

Our emphasis on combating imperialism and hegemonism and developing the national economy and culture as the primary way of solving the population problem does not imply that in our view a population policy is of no consequence. Here we would first like to point out that the formulation and implementation of population policies, the setting of population targets, the carrying out of census and the publication of statistics are entirely within the scope of the internal affairs and sovereignty of each country, which must be decided by each government in the light of the specific conditions of its own country. Some countries need to lower, and others to raise, the rate of population growth to a proper extent. No uniformity should be imposed since conditions vary from country to country. Any international technical cooperation and assistance in population matters must follow the principles of complete voluntariness of the parties concerned, strict respect for state sovereignty, absence of any strings attached and promotion of the self-reliance of the recipient countries. We are firmly opposed to the superpowers intervening by any means in the population policy of other countries on the pretext of what they call "population explosion" or "over-population." We are firmly opposed to the attempt of some international organizations to infringe on the sovereignty of recipient countries by conditioning aid on restricting their population growth rate.

After overthrowing the rule of the imperialists and their lackeys, we in China have secured the prerequisites for the planned development of the national economy as well as the planned regulation of the rate of population growth. On the basis of energetically developing production and raising the living standards of the people, China has developed medical and health services throughout the cities and countryside and strengthened the work of maternity and child care, thus reducing mortality on the one hand and regulating the birthrate through birth planning on the other. Our birth planning is not merely birth control, as some people understand it to be, it comprises different measures for different circumstances. In densely populated areas, late marriage and birth control are encouraged on the basis of voluntariness, while active treatment is given in cases of sterility. In national minority areas and other sparsely populated areas, appropriate measures are taken to facilitate population growth, while birth control advice and help are given to those parents who have too many children and desire birth control. Such a policy of planned population growth is in the interest of the thorough emancipation of women and the proper bringing up of future generations as well as of national construction and prosperity. China's mortality rate has dropped by a big margin. The birthrate in densely populated areas has decreased in varying degrees. In the national minority areas, a change has been brought about in the situation prevailing in the past, in which the population grew at an extremely slow rate or even dropped sharply owing to brutal persecution by the forces of reaction—a change that has resulted in a fairly rapid increase of the population there. Of course, these are but initial achievements. We have not yet acquired adequate experience in the work of birth planning and we must continue our efforts. . . .

G. Family Planning Gains Popularity*

It has become an increasingly popular practice in China today for husband and wife to discuss family planning so that both will be in a better position to devote themselves to political activities, the study of Marxism-Leninism-Mao Tsetung Thought and the building of socialism and take part in cultural and sports activities conducive to mental and physical fitness.

A case in point is Chou Mai-chang of Peking. Formerly a housewife, she took a job to contribute her share in socialist construction in 1958 when there was a great leap forward in the national economy. She has practiced effective contraception for 17 years since she gave birth to her third child at the age of twenty-six. She said: "We revolutionary women are all for family planning without which I couldn't possibly have done well in both my studies and work these years." An energetic middle-aged woman, she is now vice-chairman of the revolutionary committee of a garment factory making pajamas for export. She is in charge of the study of Marxist-Leninist theory, political and ideological education and personnel work in the factory.

In 1958, the Party put forward the general line of "going all out, aiming high and achieving greater, faster, better and more economical results in building socialism." The people of the whole country started the great leap forward and the movement for the formation of people's communes. Anxious to do her bit, Chou Mai-chang got together several other housewives in the neighborhood and started a sewing group by pooling their own sewing machines. Later, several such sewing groups merged to set up a garment factory.

Peking Review, No. 38 (September 20, 1974).

"At that time I felt just like a bird out of a cage," Chou Mai-chang recalled. "I was really happy to be able to add a brick or two to the edifice of socialism."

Chou Mai-chang has a family of five. Her husband now works at the Peking Municipal Power Supply Bureau. Her eldest son, previously a member of a geological prospecting team, enrolled last year for further studies in a college on recommendation. Her second son went to work on a farm in Inner Mongolia run by a PLA reclamation corps after finishing junior middle school, and her seventeen-year-old daughter is now studying in a postal technical school in Peking.

Chou Mai-chang lives in a lane which comes under the Fengsheng Neighborhood Revolutionary Committee, one of nine such organizations in the Western District of the city of Peking. This neighborhood consists of two streets and 132 lanes, and is inhabited by 53,000 people in 14,000 families, averaging 3.75 per family. Family planning is this neighborhood epitomizes in a measure the work being done in Chinese cities. A family planning committee has been set up under the neighborhood revolutionary committee, and the 25 residents' committees under it have each a family planning leading group in charge of popularizing the significance of the work among the inhabitants. Each family is advised to have no more than two children, but this, of course, is entirely on a voluntary basis. Statistics collected by health workers show that nearly 90 percent of the over 4,000 women in the child-bearing age group in this neighborhood take regular measures of contraception. The remaining include the newlyweds and cases of infertility.

Planned population growth

A planned population growth policy is being carried out in China. On the other hand, on the basis of actively developing production and raising the people's standard of living, urban and rural medical and health work is being extensively expanded to improve medical care of mothers and children and to reduce the mortality rate. On the other hand, planned childbirth is carried out to regulate the birthrate. In this respect, measures vary with different conditions in different areas. Late marriage and birth control are encouraged in densely populated areas with a high birthrate. In other areas, such as places sparsely peopled by minority nationalities, measures conducive to population growth are taken, but advice and help are always available to those who want birth control.

At present, while family planning has been popularized in the cities, it is also being introduced in the rural areas. This is possible primarily because the Chinese people, led by the Chinese Communist Party, have overthrown the reactionary rule of imperialism, feudalism and bureaucrat-capitalism, won victory in the democratic revolution and embarked on socialist revolution and socialist construction. The all-round development of national construction has resulted in universal employment and, in particular, made it possible for large numbers of women to join in socialist construction. All this has created the basic conditions for family planning and a proper arrangement of family life. This shows that the primary way of solving the population problem is for the oppressed nations to get rid of the rule of imperialism and its lackeys, win independence, develop the national economy and national culture in an independent way and raise the people's living standards. Some people assert that only by trimming down the size of families and restricting population growth is it possible to solve the problems of unemployment, poverty and population. This is an erroneous argument which puts the cart before the horse and stands the facts on their heads.

In old China, the masses of working women, while suffering like other laboring people from oppression by the reactionary political regimes, were weighed down further by religious authority, clan authority and masculine authority. Women were regarded as "an instrument for producing children" and slaves doing household chores. They had no say in the family. Under the pernicious influence of the doctrines of Confucius and Mencius, which proclaimed that "there are three things which are unfilial, and to have no posterity is the greatest of all," women were even more discriminated against should they be infertile or fail to bring forth a male descendant.

Women have won emancipation in New China, enjoying equal political and economic rights as men and having equal opportunities to employment. A new atmosphere prevails in the families characterized by equality, democracy and unity between husband and wife who work and study together to build up the socialist motherland. This is why the long cherished aspirations of women —planned childbirth and decision on the size of the family by both husband and wife—can thus be realized today. In China, family planning is not regarded as a matter which concerns only the individuals but a major issue beneficial to socialist revolution and construction; to their own work and the training of successors to the revolutionary cause of the proletariat.

Popularization of family planning is conducted under state guidance and on a voluntary basis. Proletarian politics are put in command to enhance the people's understanding of its significance, and concrete measures are adopted, such as free operations and supply of contraceptives. Family planning is not only widely carried out in the cities, but is being practiced by more and more people in the countryside. For instance, in the Szuchiching (Evergreen) People's Commune, a well-known vegetable producer on the outskirts of Peking, family planning finds a favorable response among working women who account for half of the commune's labor force. Seventy-four percent of the more than 5,000 women in the child-bearing age group there have taken contraceptive measures.

Chi Ya-ping, chairman of the women's federation of the commune, commented on the situation: "In our commune, women are playing their full role as 'the other half' in political life and in production. In the current movement to criticize Lin Piao and Confucius, women account for about two-thirds of the 358 activists in theoretical studies and they also make up half of the vegetable growers. Of the 3,400 Party members and Communist Youth League members, 1,600 are women. Taking an active part in political life and in production, women naturally would like to be less burdened by children. That's why family planning, when popularized, is readily accepted by most women in the countryside. Of course conservative ideas and obstacles still exist, and these mainly stem from the outdated idea that boys are preferred to girls. Some parents would like to have a boy although they have already several daughters. This is nothing strange, considering the fact that the reactionary ideas of Confucius and Mencius had been dominant for more than 2,000 years."

In the Szuchiching People's Commune, a number of married women have had operations for sterilization after two or more childbirths. Some old women often advise their daughter-in-law to practice family planning. A typical example is woman commune member Hsu Shu-hsien, who has two sons. When her first daughter-in-law had two children she successfully persuaded her not to have any more. Hsu Shu-hsien recalled that in the old society her mother had ten children, but only she and her two sisters survived. She said: "Today, our people's commune has a hospital and every production brigade under it has a cooperative medical service station and every production team has its own 'barefoot doctors.' Infant mortality has been reduced to practically nil. We women are no longer downtrodden, so why shouldn't we practice family planning?"

Results gained

Through the popularization of family planning in the past few years, the rate of population growth has declined in densely populated areas. On the other hand, in areas inhabited by minority nationalities where the population was on the decrease before liberation, it has shown marked increases. In Peking and Shanghai, the rates of population growth have dropped to 9.7 and 4.8 per thousand respectively. In the streets and lanes under the Fengsheng Neighborhood Revolutionary Committee in Peking, the rate of natural population growth dropped from 6.95 per thousand in 1972 to 6.12 in 1973. In the Szuchiching People's Commune, the rate dropped from 13.35 per thousand in 1972 to 11.39 last year. In the Sinkiang Uighur Autonomous Region where the minority nationalities live in compact communities, however, the rate of natural population growth is now 30 per thousand.

Chi Ya-ping said: "China is a socialist country, and our socialist construction is carried out in a planned way. It is only natural that population should also grow in a planned way. In our country production rises much faster than population growth. This is also the case in our commune. From 1956 to 1973 the commune's population increased by 39 percent while the yield of grain jumped from 2.36 tons to 6.28 tons per hectare, an increase of 165 percent. In vegetable growing, the per-hectare yield has increased from 50.1 tons to 76.7 tons, and many varieties have been added. The commune's total income rose from over 6 million yuan to more than 21 million yuan, a 3.53-fold increase. Facts have proved the complete untenability of the argument that increases in grain output can never keep pace with population growth and that overpopulation is the root cause of poverty. Under the leadership of the Communist Party, the Chinese people overthrew the three big mountains of imperialism, feudalism and bureaucrat-capitalism and have successfully carried out socialist revolution and construction. Although China's population has been on the increase, the country is free of unemployment, national economic construction is thriving and the people's living standards are steadily rising."

H. *Tsao An-hua* / Family Planning in Jutung County*

I. Declining population growth

Jutung County in east China on the Yellow Sea coast has 94,700 hectares of cultivated land and a population of 1.065 million, averaging 669 persons per square kilometer.

It is one of the models of family planning in the country's rural areas. Since 1971 the population growth there has swiftly fallen. In 1977 its birthrate was 10.5 per thousand, mortality rate was 6.82 per thousand, so the natural increase was 3.68 per thousand; 92 percent of married couples in the country practice planned parenthood.

Before liberation working people in Jutung, like elsewhere in China, were oppressed and exploited by imperialism, feudalism and bureaucrat-capitalism, haunted by poverty and unemployment. Many died in wars, epidemics and famines.

Wei Chih-tien, sixty-year-old chairman of the county poor and lower-middle peasants' association, told me that his parents had a family prolific of children—ten brothers and sisters all told. But they did not have the means to feed them. Three of them were drowned in their infancy, another three sent to an orphanage and one died. He and two brothers who survived became landlords' laborers in their early teens. What they earned was hardly enough to keep their body and soul together. In spring when they were on short commons, if they were to borrow from the landlord a sack of grain they had to return a sack and a half after autumn harvest. Miscellaneous taxes extorted by the government (salt, tobacco, marriage, road taxes and so on) virtually bled the poor white. When cholera struck Jutung in 1936, because the reactionary gov-

*This report appeared in three consecutive issues of *Peking Review*: No. 14 (April 7, 1978), No. 15 (April 14, 1978), No. 16 (April 21, 1978).

ernment did nothing to help and the working people could not afford medical treatment, the death toll was heavy, so heavy that there weren't even enough pallbearers.

In those days the working people could hardly keep themselves alive let alone bring up children. Many children were born and many died. People called childbirth or a family with too many children an "infantile disaster."

After liberation in 1949 the feudal exploitative system was overthrown and the working people became masters of society.

Since the cooperative transformation of agriculture in 1956, particularly after the setting up of rural people's communes in 1958, the peasants of Jutung, relying on the strength of the collective, built water conservancy projects, practiced scientific farming, established farm machinery plants, chemical fertilizer plants, and built pumping stations to bring about a tremendous change in production. Life got better and "infantile disaster" was never heard of again.

Here is a table comparing the county's per-hectare yields of grain and cotton and its gross industrial and agricultural output value with the population growth for 1949 and 1976:

	1949	1976	Percentage increase
Grain	2,340 kg.	8,630 kg.	368
Cotton	67.5 kg.	788.3 kg.	1,167.8
Gross industrial and agricultural output value	67.689 million *yuan*	427.24 million *yuan*	631.2
Population	699,700	1,065,300	52.3

These figures show that the increase of material product far outpaced the population growth. Chairman Mao on the eve of nationwide liberation in 1949 said in his article "The Bankruptcy of the Idealist Conception of History" refuting a Western bourgeois economist who claimed that increases in food cannot keep pace with increases in population: "Revolution plus production." Jutung County has accomplished just that.

Here, today in Jutung, everybody has enough food, clothing and a job. Culture, education, medicine and health have all swiftly developed.

At the time of liberation Jutung had only two hospitals and 610 private doctors. In those days it was hard even to find treatment for a case of appendicitis. It now boasts 2,516 full-time medical personnel reinforced by 1,797 barefoot doctors in the production brigades who spend their time in production when not treating patients. All its people's communes today have a cooperative medical care service.* The county hospital today can handle most cases of illness.

In education, there was only one junior middle school in the whole county in 1949. In 1977 the number of senior and junior middle schools jumped to 190. By 1975 junior middle school education became universal and the following year 90 percent of junior middle school graduates were able to continue their studies in senior middle schools.

Most peasant households today have enough food and to spare and live in houses of brick with tile roofs.

Widespread family planning which began in Jutung in 1970 has borne notable results.

Why the planned population increase? Ours is a socialist country with public ownership of the means of production. The national economy develops according to plan and this requires that population increase must also take place according to plan. While man is chiefly a producer he is also a consumer. China has a vast population which is still growing. It is true the rates of growth in agriculture and industry over the past 28 years have been greater than the rate of population growth and this has ensured an increasingly better life for the people year after year, but if the population growth is slowed down somewhat then there will be more grain and other material products available for national construction and for the further betterment of the people's living standard.

Family planning also helps liberate women from onerous household chores to enable them to take a direct part in socialist construction. This is conducive to women's liberation and to socialist construction.

Family planning also improves women's health and has proved to be a boon to their children's upbringing and education.

The emphasis in planned population growth is "planning." It

---

*Cooperative medical care service is funded by production brigades from their collective welfare accumulation. Each commune member needs only pay a small annual fee to receive medical treatment with no further charges.

is more than birth control. There are two aspects to family planning. One is late marriage and the other is fewer births. By late marriage we mean young people must not get married as early as seventeen or eighteen and sometimes even fourteen or fifteen as was the practice in the past. This also means that these married couples will have children at an older age which helps control population growth.

In the rural areas men are not encouraged to get married until they have reached twenty-five and women until they are twenty-three; in the urban areas men until they have reached twenty-seven and women, twenty-five. Each couple may have no more than two children and it is encouraged that the interval between births should be reasonably extended.

Because of the introduction of family planning the natural increase of population in Jutung County fell from 17.3 per thousand in 1970 to 4 per thousand in 1975.

Family planning is encouraged only in areas of dense population. In sparsely populated national minority areas and certain other areas population growth is encouraged. Over the past 20-odd years minority nationalities in the country have registered fairly rapid increases in population. In the case of members of minority nationalities with a big family who have the wish for family planning, proper advice and facilities are provided.

II. Of the masses' own will

When in Jutung I called on a woman named Chang Fu-mei of the Tungtien Commune. Married to a widower in 1962, she lived happily with her husband and two stepdaughters. Although she was entitled to have children of her own, she had chosen, with the husband's consent, to take contraceptive measures.

Asked if she didn't mind that she did not have children of her own, she replied: "Family planning is a very significant matter for the whole country and children are, first of all, successors to the revolution. What difference does it make if the girls I mother are not of my own?"

Chang was one of the many selfless persons I knew in Jutung where planned birth has been welcomed by the many.

When twenty-year-old Shan Yung-li of the Hsinyao Commune came back home upon her graduation from senior middle school, she became an agro-technician in the production team she belonged to. Some young men were taken up with her but she preferred to acquire more knowledge when young and marry at an older age as the state had called on the young people to do. Now the production team Shan worked in was a large cotton-producer, where lady-birds were needed to bring the cotton aphis under control. But they had to be brought in from the south every spring because of the cold winter there. So the local agricultural institute suggested that Shan should find out a way for these bugs to live in the locality through the winter. Night and day Shan spent her time in the laboratory breeding these bugs and finally found the way. She made rapid progress in her studies and came to the fore in productive labor. In 1975 she was admitted into the Chinese Communist Party and became the deputy secretary of the production brigade Party branch. Now twenty-seven she will soon get married.

I also knew a Liu Mei-ying of the Chanan Commune who got married at nineteen and gave birth to a daughter the following year. When the commune called on its married members to practice planned parenthood in 1970, she decided that she would not have her second child until after her first one was nine. Her mother-in-law, who wished to have a grandson at an earlier date, at first wasn't happy about the idea. It was Liu Mei-ying who patiently persuaded the old lady to her point of view. This year the second son of the family also got married and planned to have a child next year. The mother-in-law again urged Liu Mei-ying to have her next baby in the same year so that she could help bring them up together. Liu Mei-ying again persuaded her mother-in-law to give up the idea.

Family planning in Jutung County did not come easily.

Breaking down old ideas

Although family planning is conducive to the planned development of the socialist economy and to women's health and their children's upbringing, not many people could appreciate all these at the first onset. Many people, bound by old ideas, preferred boys to girls, thinking that only the former could carry on the family line. They may already have several daughters but still wished to have a son and this was one main reason why there were so many children in a family.

In introducing family planning, there must be a rupture with traditional ideas, involving a large amount of work in publicity accompanied by effective measures.

Accordingly, cadres from the county Party committee down consider this a matter of first importance, put it on the order of the day and check up work in this field as they do in other fields. The success or failure in the work of family planning is also considered as one of the essential factors in commending advanced individuals and collectives.

The county government and its grass-roots administrative units have set up special organizations to give publicity and guidance to family planning. In a production brigade and above there is a special board of family planning to be headed by a Party secretary and composed of leading members of the revolutionary committee, the women's federation, the Communist Youth League and the public health department. In a production team there is also a group of people in charge.

Publicity on family planning is given in various ways so that its significance is made known to each and every peasant household. The county rediffusion station and blackboard bulletins in the production teams are used to further this end while the county literary and art troupe often gives special performances in factories and villages with family planning as their theme.

In Jutung there are 70,000 people taking part in the work of propagating and advising on family planning, most of them being workers and peasants who do the job in their spare time voluntarily.

Family planning involves hundreds of thousands of people who see things in different lights. A generalized call often does not serve the purpose; there should be a more personal approach and different people should be dealt with in different ways.

There was a woman named Kuo Yueh who had given birth to five children and had nine abortions before liberation and had two more children after liberation. Too many childbirths made her hair turn grey in her early thirties. She often used her own bitter experience to persuade young people to marry at an older age and practice family planning after marriage. Taking her advice, not a single married couple in the production team which she belonged to had failed in subscribing to planned parenthood. Last year when she went to see her son working somewhere else, she gave the same advice to her daughter-in-law. Her youngest daughter was not married until twenty-five.

Chang Wang-ying, an activist in propagating family planning, used to be a go-between, with a ready tongue whiling the time away without doing anything useful, before she became the leader of a women's team. When the work of family planning got started, Chang Mei-ying, director of the commune's women's federation, helped her to see that she was wrong in spreading the feudal idea of "getting married when you are young so that you can have a son early." Chang Mei-ying also encouraged Chang Wang-ying to do physical labor and in a year she earned 1,800 work-points, instead of 200 as in the previous year. Once she got used to physical labor, she grew to like it and quit her old job as a go-between. Now she used her eloquence to convince young people of the advantage of late marriage and was lauded by the masses.

III. Measures and results

Living with Wife's Family. In China's countryside there is still the old idea that daughters are "tipped out" like used water—of no more use to the family once they are married. Only sons are expected to support the parents in their old age and only sons can inherit property. The property of those without a son then goes to a nephew of the same clan. Married men going to live with their parents-in-law in the old days were targets of ridicule and discrimination and were frequently driven away over the issue of inheriting property. This view is still alive with many people so that couples already with several daughters still want a son.

Jutung County constantly propagates the idea that daughters too should support their parents in their old age and encourages men to marry girls with no brothers and to go and live with their in-laws. There is a regulation made by the county that husbands moving in to live with their parents-in-law must be considered native members of that community and must not be discriminated against.

I called in on one family in the Chapei People's Commune which had only a daughter in each four generations. All four sons-in-law lived with the wife's family. Chi Fang-chen, the fourth generation, has only a daughter (in primary school) but she is not keen on having another child—son or daughter—yet. Altogether there are seven in her family, a great grandmother, grandmother, mother,

father, husband and daughter. They are provided with food, clothing, housing and medical care, a standard of living not lower than
that of an average peasant in the locality, by the communes. Cadres
and commune members often help them with chores about their
house. Hence the peasants see that only the socialist system is the
basic guarantee for a happy, carefree old age.

Free Contraceptives. Various contraceptive measures are available free of charge to the people, contraceptive devices and pills
are brought to the masses at their homes by cadres, medical workers
and members of family planning propaganda and advising groups.

If a contraceptive measure is requested (including ligation of
spermatic duct, tubal ligation, induced abortion and insertion or
removal of intrauterine devices) the state will pay all expenses including hospitalization fees.

Medical workers are being constantly trained and their skills
improve all the time. Over the past eight years the Chanan Commune Public Health Center did some 2,000 operations without a
mishap. I saw a tubal ligation done by two doctors in 10 minutes.

Peasants and workers who have such operations are allowed several days of leave with full pay.

Flexibility. In Jutung County, a maximum of two children per
family is encouraged but exceptions are made for those with handi-
capped children.

While Tsao Mei-fang of the Chanan Commune was busily nursing
her elder child in hospital for a heart disease, she forgot to take
her pills and later started her third baby. She asked for an abortion
but the doctor the commune health center sent to her home found
that her elder child had a congenital heart disease, so abortion was
ruled out for Tsao. Later, the child died and Tsao had her third
child. Then her request for tubal ligation was granted.

Protection of Women and Children. Since 1970, Jutung County
has been conducting extensive check-ups among women and popularizing health and hygiene knowledge during menstruation, pregnancy, parturition and breast-feeding. Women today in Jutung have
good health habits, and much has been accomplished in preventing
certain women's diseases. Over the past six or seven years occur-
rence of certain diseases has fallen 50 percent. Modern midwifery
is the rule in the county and since 1975 there has been no case of
tetanus of the newborn or puerperal fever.

In the county rural areas kindergartens and nurseries have been widely set up. Production team nurseries accept children under three years old and production brigade kindergartens care for children between three and seven. The expenses of the kindergartens and nurseries are paid out of the collective's public welfare fund. In 1977, 53.4 percent of the county's children were in nurseries and 87.8 percent in kindergartens. Teachers and nurses teach the children good health habits, and pay attention to improving children's health. As the children grow up healthily, the parents are no longer worried and do not wish to have a lot of children.

What Family Planning Accomplished. Family planning in Jutung County has proved beneficial in many aspects.

In the past, women with five or six children were burdened with onerous household chores and reduced to mere drudges.

Now, with only two children and an extended interval between births and with nurseries and kindergartens to lighten the family's burden of looking after them, a woman spends less time looking after babies and more time for work, study and social activities.

Farming needs a lot of manpower. Prior to 1965, the turnout rate of able-bodied women participating in labor was 75 percent because of too many children and onerous household chores. Since family planning was introduced in 1970, women in the county have fewer children and many more are able to take part in collective production. The turn-out rate in 1976 was 96 percent—the 4 percent represented monthly, nursing, pregnancy and confinement leave.

Women take part in sowing, field management and harvesting together with men. They do up to 90 percent of the work in cotton fields. The men are engaged mainly in leveling the land, digging canals and shoulder-pole work. In the old days no woman in fishing communes went out to sea to fish, but today women accompany the men out at sea for two to three months at a stretch. Those who stay home fish along the coast.

As a result of participation in revolution and production as well as study of politics and culture, women enhance their political consciousness and abilities. Many have become agrotechnicians, tractor or truck drivers, barefoot doctors and workers. And there are more and more women cadres and teachers in the county.

Having children later, less children and extending the interval between births are a boon to women's health and their babies. Fewer babies mean better care and better babies. Children can now all go to school; usually they can finish junior middle school.

Family planning also helps raise living standards. At the Yellow Sea Fishing Brigade, I was told by its Party branch secretary that in 1966 the brigade had to subsidize at least a dozen families who were having a tough time economically because of too many children. By 1976 only one family, because of illness and the children attending school, required help. With one half of the investment coming from the public welfare fund and the rest from the fishermen, the brigade put up two two-storied buildings to house 20 families in the brigade.

Planned control of population growth cuts down the consumption of material wealth of society and provides more materials for the expanded reproduction of the state and collective.

In 1965 the county's birth rate was 34.66 per thousand and the population growth was upwards of 25 per thousand. Since family planning was introduced, between 1972 and 1976, there were 20,000 fewer births annually than in 1965, that is, 100,000 less in five years, which meant a great saving in grain and materials.

Planned population growth is something quite new. In a letter to K. J. Kautsky, Engels predicted that there would be the abstract possibility, that the population would grow so big, that its increase would have to be limited. But when communist society had to deal with the population growth just as it dealt with the production of materials, it and it alone would be able to do so without any difficulty.

Inheriting the Marxist theory on population, Chairman Mao put forward the policy of planned population growth. Socialist China today is turning this "abstract possibility" of limiting the population increase into concrete, practical action.

I. Kao Yun and Hsiang Jung / Mongolian Population: From Steady Decline to Steady Increase*

What impressed us most, during our tour of the Inner Mongolian pastoral areas, were the children and adolescents of the Mongolian nationality. There were great numbers of them. This is a major change which means much to the areas inhabited by the Mongolians in compact communities where proverbially, "children are as rarely seen as stars in a daylight sky."

Like the other minority nationalities, the Mongolians declined sharply in numbers in old China. According to historical records, there was a population of 400,000 in what is today's Ikh Chao League," western Inner Mongolia, in the early period of the Ching dynasty (1664-1911); but by 1949 only 80,000 were left. The Mongolian nationality as a whole at that time was on the brink of extinction.

Liberation arrested the serious decline and created conditions for a steady increase in the Mongolian population. According to the autonomous region's statistical Bureau, the population today is 2.3 times the 1949 figure.

What, then, accounts for this tremendous change?

Social system has changed

We interviewed Alatanchichike, an old woman in her seventies, during our stay in the Paiyinhsile Brigade of the Szutzuwang Banner, central Inner Mongolia. She had begun herding livestock for a herdowner at the age of ten and toiled for decades, but by the time of liberation she had not earned enough for a yurt to shelter her family. In those miserable days, she lived in an enclosure made

*Peking Review, No. 47 (November 18, 1977).

of dried sheep turds and roofed with ragged felt. To kill the pangs of hunger, she scavenged dead animals and odds and ends of mutton and beef discarded by the rich. She had to give her only son to another family.

Liberation brought Alatanchichike a new lease on life. With help from the People's Government soon after liberation, she had for the first time in her life acquired a yurt she could comfortably live in and 15 sheep at her own disposal. She joined a mutual-aid team and then a cooperative and later became a member of the people's commune. Her life is improving steadily. The son she was forced to part with has returned to the family and is now a production brigade cadre as well as a "barefoot" veterinary. There are seven members in her family. The eldest of her four grandsons is already a ten-year-old primary school pupil. With earnings from their own labor, they had built themselves a spick-and-span three-room house and pitched a new yurt beside it.

"Paiyinhsile" means "rich pasture" in the Mongolian language. But in the old society only the local exploiting classes—mostly herdowners who owned over 90 percent of the 2,000 head of livestock before liberation—were rich. Wielding the power in their grip, they unscrupulously oppressed and exploited the poor herdsmen, who fared the same as beasts of burden.

Since liberation the formerly poverty-stricken herdsmen have become masters of this pastureland, with local power firmly in their control. Sujungchapu, the son of a poor herdsman, has become not only the brigade Party branch secretary but also a vice-secretary of the Party committee of the Ulan Chap League. Economically the herdsmen were also emancipated. The brigade now owns 29,700 head of livestock, 15 times the total immediately after liberation. The income of the brigade last year amounted to 260,000 *yuan*, or triple the figure of 1966, the year the Great Cultural Revolution began. Monthly income for a herdsman from collective labor exceeds what he earned in a whole year's toil before liberation. Ninety-eight percent of the commune members have moved into houses built by the brigade with the collective fund. A cooperative medical service manned by barefoot doctors has been introduced to the brigade. Over 95 percent of all school-agers are attending school. It is only today that Paiyinhsile can be called a "rich pasture" in the real sense of the words.

Paiyinhsile is 500 square kilometers in size. Now its Mongolian population of 290 is six times that immediately after liberation when there were only 45 Mongolians in 17 households, averaging barely one person for every 10 square kilometers. Youngsters under the age of fifteen today number 50 as against only two when the area was liberated.

What we saw in the brigade represents a microcosm of Inner Mongolia as a whole. Under the leadership of the Party, the Mongolian people toppled the old social system and established a socialist new one. Socialism, by liberating the productive forces, brought about rapid expansion in animal husbandry. The vigorous development of production has not only ensured an increasingly better livelihood for the herdsmen but also helped improve public medical service and promote cultural undertakings. With the popularization of knowledge about hygiene and mass participation in various sports activities, the people's health has shown vast improvement. All this has contributed to a rapid growth in population.

Population policy

Reactionary rulers in old China enforced a policy of great-Han chauvinism against the Mongolian and other minority nationalities. They discriminated against the minority people, suppressed them, and even massacred them in large numbers in a vain attempt to quell their resistance. By contrast, the Communist Party of China follows a policy of equality for all nationalities, big and small alike. In the case of Inner Mongolia, the People's Government has adopted effective measures to help the Mongolians develop their economy and culture and increase their population.

New China follows a policy of planned population growth on the basis of planned development of social production in order to protect mothers and children, better educate the younger generation and improve the people's health. But requirements for the Hans who already have a big population are different from those for the other numerically smaller nationalities. Late marriage and family planning are encouraged among the Han residents in Inner Mongolia as elsewhere in China, while effective measures have been adopted to facilitate the growth of the Mongolian population. On the other hand, if a woman of Mongolian nationality who has had many children or who is in poor health requests it, she is given birth control advice.

"Child of the Party"

As a result of economic and cultural backwardness, many diseases, especially venereal diseases (mainly syphilis and gonorrhea) spread unchecked in the preliberation Inner Mongolia. We learned this from Liu Yi-hua, a doctor who has been working there since early postliberation days to eliminate VD. Citing statistics from a local survey, he told us that at the time of liberation 57 percent of the Mongolians were suffering from venereal diseases. The rate of sterility among those women afflicted was 30 percent, while the incidence of miscarriages, premature births and stillbirths went as high as 13 percent. The mortality rate for babies with congenital syphilis reached 49 percent. VD was thus the most responsible, direct cause for the drastic decrease in population. A folk rhyme current at the time had it that "half the women never conceive; sometimes pregnant women are seen, but seldom or never newborn babies."

Beginning from 1950 medical and health departments in Inner Mongolia have focused their efforts on treating and preventing venereal diseases. Experiments were made with the aim of working out ways and means to cure the patients. The Peking Medical College also sent its students and faculty members to the autonomous region where they joined the local medical workers in two mobile medical teams to go the round in the pastoral areas. When the team in which Liu Yihua served arrived at the Szutzuwang Banner, the head of the banner himself accompanied it to the outlying rural areas. The herdsmen had had their fill of suffering from venereal diseases, but owing to their lack of scientific knowledge and the influence of the old idea that whether or not one was ill or could bear a child was all predestined, they doubted if the doctors could cure them. The bad elements also spread falsehoods to sabotage the work. Under the circumstances, the medical workers' first job was one of education among the masses to drive home the harm and origin of VD. As a result, some banished their doubts and applied for treatment. After one to three courses of treatment, lasting about three weeks, some of the patients were cured. They then became the most convincing arguments, so that others also gave up their reservations and came forward for treatment in all eagerness. In this way the medical teams toured from place to place providing medical services free of charge.

"When the herdsmen were cured," Liu recalled, "they were very grateful to the doctors, and presented the medical teams with flags to express their gratitude to the Party and Chairman Mao for sending them the doctors." "They insisted on presenting us with their fattest sheep, the best milk and other dairy food," he added. It usually took a long time to explain that the people's doctors would not receive any gifts and that this was a discipline before the herdsmen would leave, their eyes moist with grateful tears. Many patients after regaining their health, had children, and some of the babies were named "Naminhu," meaning "child of the Party," as an expression of the herdsmen's thanks to the Party.

Facilities for preventing and treating VD were set up in 1956 at the autonomous regional level and in all the leagues as well as banners and counties. Thanks to extensive and regular physical checkups and treatment over the years, VD has been eliminated throughout the region.

Maternity and child care

During our stay in the pastoral area of the Ulan Chap League we visited Chanteng, a woman herder. She wore her years so well that without her self-introduction, we would not have known her as a fifty-five-year-old. Before liberation three of her first four children died because of unhygienic methods of delivery and she herself fell prey to diseases. Since liberation she has had seven babies, all delivered with aseptic midwifery followed by plenty of nutritious food. Among her eight sons and daughters, three are married, one has joined the People's Liberation Army, three others are in school and the youngest is a bouncing seven-year-old.

The misery Chanteng experienced was the common lot of all the Mongolian laboring women before liberation. Giving birth was once looked upon as "filthy," and in some areas was not allowed in yurts, because it was said, that would "offend the spirits." A woman in labor had to go out into the open or into the sheep pens to give birth, with the result that many of them contracted puerperal fever and the infants often died of tetanus. Antenatal and postnatal rest was out of the question, as Mongolian women engaged in livestock-breeding had to shoulder heavy physical labor. This, coupled with malnourishment, gave lying-in mothers little chance of recuperation. The babies' health also suffered from lack of good nourishment.

Since liberation, large numbers of midwives capable of performing aseptic deliveries with strictly sterilized equipment have been trained, while those midwives from the old society have been taught new delivery methods. During the periods of menstruation, gravidity and breastfeeding, women receive due consideration and are assigned lighter work. Lying-in mothers are given enough time for convalescence. Infants are fed according to scientific methods and receive vaccinations and inoculations against communicable diseases. Maternity wards have been set up in many production brigades, where the midwives do regular prenatal checkups, carefully help the mothers during childbirth and look after those who rest for 15 to 20 days before going home. Of the 106 childbirths a brigade-run maternity ward in the East Uchumucin Banner has handled since 1965, not a case of puerperal fever or tetanus occurred. The rate of infant viability reached 100 percent and all the newborn babies are healthy and thriving.

Medical and health care services were extremely inadequate for the herdsmen in the preliberation days. By 1946 there were only 33 hospitals, poorly equipped and totaling less than 400 beds in the autonomous region. The situation has greatly changed today. There are now medical institutions in some localities specializing in endemic, infectious or occupational diseases and tuberculosis; and hospitals, health and disease-prevention stations, maternity and child-care centers and pharmaceutical companies have been set up not only at the autonomous regional level but also in all the leagues as well as banners and counties. Clinics have been set up in all the people's communes, and cooperative medical service has been organized in upwards of 95 percent of the production brigades. The commune members, on payment of a small annual premium, enjoy free medical care. The whole region now has 16,000 barefoot doctors, averaging two or three in every production brigade. The average life expectancy of the Mongolians has gone up from nineteen before liberation to sixty-four today.

Transforming old customs

Long-standing backwardness of production, poverty, and lack of culture and education were the basis of many unsanitary living habits in the old society. Nursing and sick animals used to be kept in the yurts together with the herdsmen, as there were no barns, stables or pens. Inside, the yurts were blackened by the grime and smoke of years, and threadbare blankets spread over the ground served as beds for the families. Just outside was the livestock yard, littered with dung. As a result of penetrating moisture, many herders suffered from rheumatism and lumbago, and sterility was not uncommon among the women.

In compliance with Chairman Mao's teaching: "Get mobilized, pay attention to hygiene, reduce disease, improve health conditions," the local herdsmen launched mass environmental sanitation campaigns after liberation.

We paid a visit to a settlement of the Shajutala Production Brigade in the Abaka Banner. Herdsmen's houses and yurts were arranged in a neat row. One hundred meters to the leeward side were barns and pens for the animals; while about 50 meters windward were parked some carts loaded with tanks of drinking water fetched from nearby wells. The surroundings were tidy and clean.

On entering the yurts we found things equally neat and clean. Stoves were fixed with stacks and food utensils carefully washed so that they gleamed. With wooden floors, the yurts were free of moisture.

When dusk set in, the cattle were herded back from the day's grazing. Pails in hand, wearing clean work overalls, women went to milk the cows. When it came to delivering lambs and calves, we were told requirements for sterilization were even stricter.

Tungtehpu, a herdsman, lived with his family in a roomy, well-ventilated single-storied house where conditions of hygiene were better than in a yurt. He told us that in bygone days lambs and calves were delivered in the yurts and that in doing this work he and many others had fallen victim to brucellosis, a disease caused by bacteria from the animal's placenta. In his brigade 21 percent of the people had contracted the disease. After liberation, all the patients were cured and no new cases have occurred, thanks to constant medical checkups and treatment given by the mobile medical teams and to the periodic mass sanitation campaigns. Hale and hearty at the age of fifty-two, Tungtehpu is now working as a horse herder for the brigade. Though his was a painstaking job he worked tirelessly. Beaming with confidence he said to us: "I intend to go on herding the collective's horses for many, many more years!"

About the Editor

A graduate of Haverford College, H. Yuan Tien received an M.A. in Sociology from the University of Pennsylvania and a Ph.D. in Demography from the Australian National University. He has taught at various universities in the United States, at the Australian National University and at the University of Hong Kong, and he is now Professor of Sociology at The Ohio State University. From 1969 to 1972 Dr. Tien was the director of the Institute of Comparative Sociology, and from June 1979 to March 1980 he did research in the People's Republic of China as a Senior Research Scholar of the Committee on Scholarly Exchange with the People's Republic of China, National Academy of Sciences.

Dr. Tien has delivered and published a wide variety of papers on demography and related subjects, especially with respect to China, and he is the author of *Social Mobility and Controlled Fertility* (1965) and *China's Population Struggle: Demographic Decisions of the People's Republic, 1949-1969* (1973) and the editor (with Frank Bean) of *Comparative Family and Fertility Research* (1974).